LIFT YOUR SAILS

The Challenge of Being a Christian

Vincent Dwyer, o.c.s.o.

AN IMAGE BOOK
DOUBLEDAY
NEW YORK   LONDON   TORONTO   SYDNEY   AUCKLAND

An Image Book
Published by Doubleday, a division of Bantam Doubleday Dell
Publishing Group, Inc., 666 Fifth Avenue, New York, New York 10103.

Image, Doubleday and the portrayal of a cross intersecting a circle
are trademarks of Doubleday, a division of Bantam Doubleday Dell
Publishing Group, Inc.

Acknowledgments appear on page vi.

Library of Congress Cataloging-in-Publication Data
Dwyer, Vincent. 1928–
Lift your sails.
1. Spiritual life—Catholic authors. I. Title.
BX2350.2.D89   1987   248.4'82   87–6839

ISBN 0-385-24257-3 (pbk.)

BG

CONTENTS

Grateful acknowledgment is made to the following for permission to quote from previously published material:

Cistercian Publications for excerpts from Aelred of Rievaulx: *On Spiritual Friendship*, translated by Mary Eugenia Laker, SSND, copyright © 1977 and used with their permission.

Darton, Longman & Todd, Ltd., and Doubleday & Company, Inc., for excerpts from The New Jerusalem Bible, copyright © 1985 and used with permission of the publisher.

Doubleday & Company, Inc., for excerpts from *The Cloud of Unknowing*, edited by William Johnston, an Image Books original, copyright © 1973 and used with permission of the publisher.

Harcourt Brace Jovanovich, Inc., for excerpts from *The Four Loves* by C. S. Lewis, copyright © 1960 by Helen Joy Lewis and used with permission of the publisher.

Jossey Bass Publishing, Inc., for excerpts from *Measuring Ego Development* by J. Loevinger, J. Wessler, and C. Redmore, copyright © 1970 and used with permission of the publisher.

Macmillan Publishing Company for excerpts from *Between Man and Man* by Martin Buber, copyright © 1965; and *New Theology #2* by M. Marty and D. G. Peerman, copyright © 1965. Used with permission of the publisher.

Paulist Press for excerpts from *On Prayer* by Karl Rahner, © 1958 and used with permission of the publisher.

Sheed & Ward for excerpts from *Christ the Sacrament of God*, edited by Denis O'Callaghan, copyright © 1964 and used with permission of the publisher.

Sheed & Ward for excerpts from *Christ the Sacrament of the Encounter with God* by Edward Schillebeeckx, copyright © 1963 and used with permission of the publisher.

Sheed & Ward for excerpts from *Sin, Liberty, and Law* by Louis Monden, copyright © 1965 and used with permission of the publisher.

United States Catholic Conference for excerpts from the English translation of *Ecclesiam Suam* (Paths of the Church) by Pope Paul VI, copyright © 1964; *The Lord and Giver of Life* by Pope John Paul II, copyright © 1986; and *Sects or New Religious Movements: Pastoral Challenge*, copyright © 1986. Used with permission of the publisher.

ings to their family, and I hope that this book will bring
the "Good News" to many.

I'm grateful to have the opportunity to thank the many
who have shaped and influenced me on my own journey.
I'm indebted to my family, especially to my mother and
father. The community that I grew up in was indeed
special, and I have come to appreciate it more deeply as
the years have passed. My years in the Navy had a profound impact on me. The men with whom I served on the
U.S.S. *Flying Fish*, SS229, taught me about friendship,
commitment, responsibility; they turned my life around.
They gave me above all self-confidence and a taste of
community—many of them became "family" for me. St.
Anselm's College gave me the opportunity to ground my
faith and stimulated my search for truth. The monks there
taught me much about the spiritual life, and through their
example they whetted my appetite for a monastic life. I'm
most grateful to Abbot Gerald McCarthy, who had a profound impact on my life. The time that I spent working
with the Daughters of Charity introduced me to the rich
spirituality of St. Vincent de Paul, which led me to take his
name as a religious. To the Sisters of Charity of New York,
and to Monsignor Michael Dwyer, my spiritual director,
along with those with whom I worked, I say thanks. My
own community of St. Joseph's Abbey has enriched my
life and provided me the opportunity of discovering so
many of the riches of our heritage. My days at Catholic
University enriched my life in an incredible way, and the
professors I had opened my life in a way that was profound. The academic life at the University of North Carolina in Charlotte, St. Mary's College in Winona, and the
University of Notre Dame provided me with an opportunity to explore my dreams. The interaction with students
and my colleagues tested and expanded my assumptions.

It was in this environment that I conceived the idea and finally founded the Center for Human Development.

The Center for Human Development has touched the lives of countless thousands through its various programs serving those in ministry. Our multimedia programs, especially Genesis II, have touched millions in the English-speaking world. All of this great work could not have taken place without the support of many. The distinguished men and women who have served on our Board of Directors have enriched the vision of the Center and made much of our work happen. Without the dedicated men and women who have staffed the Center over these many years, and the hundreds who have been Associates, helping us in our ministry, we could never have touched the lives of so many. I'm indebted to the staff in a special way for putting up with my "quirks," supporting and encouraging me. It might not be quite so obvious to those to whom we have ministered, but I must say that those to whom I have been able to minister have, in turn, often without fully knowing it, ministered to me and enriched my life.

I thank the Board of Directors in a special way for having given me a sabbatical in recognition of my Silver Jubilee of priesthood. This time has allowed me to step back, to study, to reflect, and to pray. I have spent much of my free time here in Europe. I settled in Florence, where I actually finished the book. I'm grateful to a priest friend who lived with me during those months. In the evenings we sat at the top of the "hermitage," which overlooked all of Florence, and shared our dreams about the priesthood and the Church. So often those sharing sessions and prayer opened me when I was stuck and the work began to flow again. The time in Florence turned out to be one of the most creative periods on my journey. The Board of

INTRODUCTION

For the past thirty some years, I've been a member of the community of St. Joseph's Abbey in Spencer, Massachusetts. Twenty-five of those years have been as a priest. In the late sixties, I became ill and it was determined that my medical problems made it impossible for me to continue living the strict Trappist life, and I was given a medical leave of absence from my community. In 1969, I completed my doctorate in Sacred Theology at Catholic University of America. My major area of concentration during my doctoral program was in Spirituality. In 1972, I founded the Center for Human Development in order to respond to the need for spiritual renewal in the Church. For the past fifteen years, I have been giving retreats, workshops, and lectures to priests, religious, and laypeople concerning the Christian message—its meaning and relevance in our day. During that time, I have had the privilege of being invited to share in the intimate drama of a great number of human hearts. This book rises out of, and is the fruit of, these experiences and reflections on my own journey.

One of the gifts that has been mine is to have seen time

and time again the extraordinary power of forgiveness and love. There is no human experience that can compare to that of a soul who, through human understanding and reconciliation, begins to taste the cosmic and all-embracing love of God. One of my goals in writing this book is to unleash our potential to love, to forgive, and to grow.

The message of love and forgiveness is as old and older than Christianity. In fact, it is timeless. But eternal wine must always be placed in new temporal bottles because of the vicissitudes of time: new ways must always be sought to speak about and to realize these changeless realities. Like any perspective, mine is not ultimate, or perfect, or complete; it is simply the vision I have been granted on my own journey. Furthermore, the reality of love is as expansive as the universe itself, going far beyond the dogmatic boundaries of Christianity. It is the beating heart in all that lives, and all religions in one way or another address themselves to it. Yet my tradition is the Catholic Church and its teachings, and visions are my life and the marrow of my being. When I speak of God's love I cannot but speak of the revelation of Jesus Christ. Thus, this book and its language are intended for those who have accepted the message of Christ and who are trying to follow Him.

Our times have witnessed the breakdown of traditional all-embracing religious forms and their replacement by all sorts of partial and fragmentary ideologies. There is an aching hunger in the "streets" of our time—a hunger for meaning! In the front ranks of those who have tried to address the problem of human meaning are the behavioral scientists. Some of their insights are helpful in bringing to the surface and recasting our rich Christian heritage. I firmly believe that our spiritual heritage has much to offer in constructively facing our existential predicament.

Today we find an enormous amount of literature dealing with human growth and development. This body of knowledge can be a tremendous tool in understanding our journey to the Father, a journey that begins at birth and ends only in death. This lifelong journey is often referred to as a process of education or formation. However you wish to describe it, one must recognize that it is of paramount importance. Education, as we all know, can take place in many ways, and since this is a book of words and thoughts, you'll find at the end of each chapter a list of suggested reflections and readings which can help you to wade further into the stream.

From my early days, I asked many questions in search for meaning and methods to live an exciting life—a life that would in some way make a difference. When I was very young, a very dear and holy person in my parish gave me "The Parable of The Pilgrim," by the fourteenth-century English mystic Walter Hilton. I found it interesting, but it seemed too simple and some of its language had little meaning to my understanding of life. It now has great meaning as I grow older, and I would encourage you to reflect and pray on the following passage:

> A certain man had a great desire to go to Jerusalem. Not knowing the right way, he inquired of one he hoped could direct him, and asked by what path he could reach there in safety. The other said, "The journey there is long and full of difficulties. There are several roads that appear and promise to lead there, but their dangers are too great. However, I know one way which, if you will faithfully follow according to the marks and directions that I shall give you, will certainly

lead you there. I cannot, however, promise you security from any frights, beatings, and other ill-usages and temptations of all kinds; yet, if you only have courage and patience enough to suffer them, but pass on quietly having this only in your mind, and sometimes on your tongue, 'I am nothing, I have nothing, I desire only one thing, and that is the love of our Lord Jesus, and to be with him at peace in Jerusalem,' I believe in due time you will get there in safety."[1]

When we respond to Christ's invitation to follow Him, we set out on a journey. Our journey is filled with mystery —pain, suffering, misunderstandings, hurts, disappointments, joys, successes and, at times, happiness, and a sense of fulfillment. These words describe, in varying ways, the ups and downs, the peaks of the mountains and also the valleys—they describe life, our own personal journey. You can describe this in different ways, but I view it as a spiritual adventure: life is meant to be not boring, but an exciting challenge. For me, God is life! He reveals Himself through persons, the Church, events—He can be found in everyday life. I see the struggle of the spiritual life as a challenge to respond to His revelation, a revelation that takes place from moment to moment. Spirituality is then the integrating focus for all aspects of growth and change. Your unique response to God revealing Himself on your journey is what it's all about. Your journey is not an isolated part of your life; it involves your whole being: spiritually, emotionally, physically, and intellectually. It is then a lifelong process that requires your personal commitment to the process of growth, which will require change and conversion in reaching the fullness of your gifts and talents—in knowing and tasting not only your own unique beauty but also the love of God!

Catholic tradition holds that each of us is blessed with many gifts and talents, and that we are called to realize and experience the fullness of these gifts. We often, consciously and unconsciously, set up obstacles, or limit ourselves by the way in which we live our lives. We can develop a particular mind-set and concentrate on surviving rather than in fully living, and it is necessary to deal with such fundamental issues such as self-image and the realization of our gifts before we can arrive at a deeper level of spirituality. I believe that while the heart of spirituality is deeply rooted in the Gospel, the manner in which a person lives out the Gospel is within the context of one's own particular time and culture. Karl Rahner stated, "Truly realized Christianity is always the achieved synthesis on each occasion of the message of the gospel and the grace of Christ, on the one hand, and the concrete situation in which the gospel is to be lived on the other."[2]

In 1955, I entered St. Joseph's Abbey in Spencer, Massachusetts, believing that I would spend the rest of my life living the simple existence of a Trappist monk. Leaving the world of my family, friends, and work was quite difficult, but I was convinced that God had called me to the monastic life. Until I entered the monastery, I had searched for God, and when I seemingly found Him I was unable or unwilling to walk on the path with Him. He never gave up on me and so, on that great day of my life when I made my solemn vows before my monastic community, I thought that I had arrived! Life would now be stable, secure, full of meaning, and I would be supported on my journey by men who had made the same commitment. When my health gave way, and following the advice of a specialist, the abbot decided that I should pursue graduate courses at Catholic University, my whole world seemed to fall apart.

I remember so well the feelings that came over me when I was told of the decision. I looked out my window in Massachusetts General Hospital in Boston and my heart cried out, Why? The road that led to the monastery had been one of ups and downs—an incredible struggle between God and my own desires. I had entered the seminary twice and left convinced that my call was to the married state. I wanted most of all to be married and to have a family, but each time I set out to achieve this goal I found myself being pulled from within. Thus, when I entered the monastery I believed that I had finally given all that I had to God and had grown over the years to love the way of life and the community in which I lived. All this was now in the past, and I was being asked to "let go" and to follow Him in a new way. Needless to say, I was scared, insecure, and frightened by the unknown. It was indeed one of the most difficult moments of my journey, and yet, as I now look back I know that it was a major turning point in my life. Although, at the time, I felt abandoned by God, yet He sustained me in spite of the terrible feelings of being all alone and having lost all that I had come to cherish so deeply. The transition from monastic life to the academic world was most challenging. Without a doubt the major hurdle I faced was to "let go" of my way of following Him and to begin anew to listening to Him in and through the unfolding events of my journey, endeavoring to respond to whatever He wanted of me.

During my years at Catholic University, I began to feel more deeply than ever before that there was a tremendous hunger to discover the rich heritage of the Church. In the midst of not only a changing world but also a changing Church, many seemed lost, confused, and searching for a way to make sense of their lives. I believed that the insights of the saints and the great men and women who had gone before us had much to offer us. Vatican II was a tremendous challenge to all of us: priests, religious, and laity. Each of us was faced with the necessity of conversion, of shifting our view points on many things that had become part of us. Like myself, perhaps you too felt that at least the Church would not change—it was the one area of our lives that gave us security. Then, it seemed, that out of nowhere the very Church that had given us so much security and sets of rules that enabled us to fulfill our duties and obligations as Catholics challenged us to "let go" and once again to become pilgrims on a journey.

During this intense period of change in the Church, priests, religious, and laity participated in all kinds of programs which were geared to updating participants and assisting them to move from the "old" to the "new." Initially, these programs of renewal were directed at the various shifts in theological perspectives, Scripture, philosophy, and other sciences. In many instances, these programs failed to "build bridges" and became sources of tension, frustration, and even division. Even today we still face the challenges of Vatican II and the urgency of helping people to find their "roots," and helping them to discover meaning in their lives is paramount.

Those of us who grew up in the pre–Vatican II Church can easily recall the difficulties that we went through as the Church began to implement changes. Many of these changes were concerned with externals rather than bringing about a conversion and renewal of the heart, a renewal of faith and the spiritual life. Changing the altar to face the people, eliminating devotions and practices which had become for many of us a way of life, left some, if not many, with a feeling of being lost. My personal experiences were verified in working with priests, religious, and laity during the late sixties and early seventies.

I became convinced that the real challenge was in the area of the internalization of the "Good News." The message of Christ and the principles of the Christian life had to be at the very heart of renewal, and to facilitate this was essential.

After completing my doctorate, I became a professor at the University of North Carolina at Charlotte. During my three years there, I began to explore ways that would enable me to create a vehicle that would respond to the internal needs of priests, religious, and laity. I finally founded the Center for Human Development in 1972 as a vehicle to respond to the spiritual hunger that I had encountered wherever I went. The task of the Center would be to surface the teachings of Christ and the great spiritual masters so that people in our times could see and know that Christ is the way, and that in Him is the true meaning of our journey. Only by turning to Christ, and responding to His invitation to follow Him, could we hope to change ourselves, the Church, and the world. I believed people wanted to grow, they wanted to know Christ, and above all they wanted to learn the art of friendship and love. The Christ event and His "Good News" is incredible—it is, as I so often say, too good to be true, but true! I wanted the world to know that the meaning of life is found in Him, and that to say "yes" to His invitation to follow Him is to set out on an exciting adventure—a great love affair!

The Center for Human Development was first established at St. Mary's College in Winona, Minnesota. The Center moved to the University of Notre Dame in Indiana in 1975, and finally in 1980 it moved to Washington, D.C. Each of the above moves was brought about by the expansion of programs and the needs of resources and interaction with other national and international organizations serving the Church. The Center, through research and development of programs, seeks to communicate the Good News of our Judeo-Christian heritage of today's Church in ways that give deeper meaning, vision, and hope.

It promotes holistic spiritual growth, integrating the Christian tradition, contemporary culture, and personal experience. It collaborates with a network of institutions and research centers throughout the world to promote, foster, and assist the renewal of the Church—the People of God.

The Ministry to Priests Program has touched the lives of over forty thousand priests in over one hundred archdioceses and dioceses throughout the English-speaking world. More than fifteen religious orders of men and women have embraced our Ministry to Religious Program. The Center also designed a program ministering to the chaplains of the U.S. military services. The Center assists seminaries and formation groups in developing programs to respond to their needs.

In 1975, I developed the program Genesis II, which was the first multimedia program designed to assist the laity in spiritual renewal. This program over the years has touched the lives of millions of people. The Center went on to develop Pathways—Journeys in Spiritual Growth, which embraces a number of individual multimedia programs being used by many to foster growth and community.

These and other programs have enabled the Center during the past fifteen years to touch the lives of many. As I look back over these many years, and the great work the Center has accomplished, I am filled with gratitude to God for all of His blessings. The contributions of outstanding individuals who have worked with me over these years have enabled the Center to continue to develop better ways of serving people.

The challenge that the Center attempted to respond to when it was founded in 1972 is, in my estimation, even more acute today, over fifteen years later. On May 3, 1986, the Vatican issued a document, *Sects or New Religious Movements: Pastoral Challenge,* which emphasizes the urgency that we face in communicating a successful rich heritage that responds to the problems people face today in their daily lives. The document places before us, under four main headings, what most of us are experiencing in family, Church, and society. Would you agree with the following analysis of the need that we are facing?

1. QUEST FOR BELONGING

The fabric of many communities has been destroyed; traditional lifestyles have been disrupted; homes are broken up; people feel uprooted and lonely. Thus the need to belong. Terms used in the responses: belonging, love, community, communication, warmth, concern, care, support, friendship, affection, fraternity, help, solidarity, encounter, dialogue, consolation, acceptance, understanding, sharing, closeness, mutuality, togetherness, fellowship, reconciliation, tolerance, roots, security, refuge, protection, safety, shelter, home.

2. SEARCH FOR WHOLENESS (HOLISM)

Many people feel that they are out of touch with themselves, with others, with their culture and environment. They experience brokenness. They have been hurt by parents or teachers, by the church or society. They feel left out. They want a religious view that can harmonize everything and everybody; worship which leaves room for body and soul, for participation, spontaneity, creativity.

3. NEED TO BE RECOGNIZED, TO BE SPECIAL
People feel a need to rise out of anonymity, to build an identity, to feel that they are in some way special and not just a number or a faceless member of a crowd. Large parishes and congregations, administration-oriented concern and clericalism, leave little room for approaching every person individually and in the person's life situation.

4. SEARCH FOR TRANSCENDENCE
This expresses a deeply spiritual need, a God-inspired motivation to seek something beyond the obvious, the immediate, the familiar, the controllable, and the material to find an answer to the ultimate questions of life and to believe in something which can change one's life in a significant way. Often the people concerned are either not aware of what the church can offer or are put off by what they consider to be a one-sided emphasis on morality or by the institutional aspects of the church.[3]

In summary, one could say that all these symptoms represent so many forms of alienation (from oneself, from others, from one's roots, culture, and so forth). The document goes on to state that "people must be helped to know themselves as unique, loved by a personal God, and with a personal history from birth through death to resurrection." It further states that "our pastoral concern should not be one dimensional; it should extend not only to the spiritual, but also the physical, psychological, social, cultural, economic, and political dimensions."

If you resonate with the above as being, as the youth say, "where it's at," then the question of how to respond in a constructive way becomes critical. It has been my personal conviction for many years that our rich heritage can respond to the "times" and that the mystics offer us insights about living life well. These insights, coupled with those of modern science, can offer each of us direction in resolving the sense of being lost and set us on the road where we can find meaning.

The title of this book, *Lift Your Sails: The Challenge of Being a Christian,* indicates that each of us has to do something. The title comes from an early Church Father who said that the task we face is to lift our sails and set out on the journey to the Heavenly Father. I was attracted to this saying because of my sailing experiences, and the image is powerful. Each of us needs to lift our own sails, pull up the anchors that we have put in place, and get on with living life, responding to Christ's invitation to follow Him.

Lift Your Sails is the fruit of years of study, research, and experiences of my own and others. It is an attempt to share with you what has deeply touched my own life, given meaning, and enabled me to discover that life can be an exciting adventure.

I ask you not to read this book just to get through it, but rather to approach it in what traditionally was called *lectio divina.* By lectio divina, I mean to put yourself in the presence of God, then *Listen,* and when something in the text hits you, let go of the book and ponder it—this will lead you to praying over your reflection. When your reflection and prayer come to an end, then resume where you left off. You'll find that by listening, reflecting, and praying over the text the integration and insights that you're looking for will come to you in and through the work of the Holy Spirit.

I pray that you'll find it a rewarding experience. The chapters provide you with the necessary steps involved in lifting your sails, and when you reach the end I hope that you'll have discovered how exciting life can be and that you'll never want to pull down your sails. In setting out on our journey we are assured by Christ that we will finally reach eternal life and in maintaining our course the English mystic Walter Hilton says, "I believe in due time you will get there in safety."

LIFT YOUR SAILS

tion, life has nothing to feed on but the daily joys and pains of work, leisure, tragedy, and comedy. And yet we know all too well that without some greater vision behind it, this alteration of light and dark, laughter and tears which we all experience becomes increasingly intolerable. When the evening news, *Time* magazine, or the economic forecast become our only indicators of reality, life can turn into despair.

Time and time again, I have seen our people, young and old, searching for some light. They want to integrate their lives, they want to live an intense Christian witness, but for the most part the reality of the Christian life remains in the shadows of past response to God's invitation to follow Him. We have given them structures, rules, guidelines which in our present day are for many no longer meaningful—they can be gathered up into a number of nice abstract truths, but they do not explore the possibilities of human potential and spiritual freedom. Each of us cries out for meaning which will allow us to reach our potential and fulfillment as a person. The meaning that is contained in the message of Christ and the insights of the mystics and saints, who have responded to His invitation to follow Him, gives to each of us the opportunity to reach our own potential and find the deepest possible fulfillment and meaning today! We need to look again, to pose new questions, to search the Scriptures and the writings of the spiritual masters for light that will offer Christians a way to provide meaning to everyday life in a world that is tossed higher and thither by every kind of "wind."

If asked as to what each of us could do to re-invite the transcendent back into our lives, I would respond: we must try to develop, by reading and reflecting, the sense of our lives as a journey—a spiritual pilgrimage. Moreover, it is the sense of the journey as a search, a search for something that has been lost or hidden but which is ours in and through Baptism—it is our very birthright! Let's consider some elements of the journey, the pilgrimage.

The Greek philosopher Socrates once said that wonder was the beginning of all wisdom. Unless we learn how to be slightly astonished over the simple fact that we are alive, over the rhythmical transformation of the seasons, our bodies and our minds, we will probably find it difficult to sense our life as a journey—a pilgrimage—an adventure. Everyone senses that he/she is on a road that begins with birth and ends in death, but everything depends upon whether one senses movement down that road as being carried along by a conveyor belt or moving consciously as an adventurer in quest of a goal and above all free to choose one's direction.

We need at times to reflect upon the passage of time in our lives and the unbelievable transformations that have occurred. Most of us have only the vague sense that we were once children, adolescents, young adults, and so on. This vague sense is coupled with the memory of a few specific incidents. But if we look more closely, we will see that even these memories are probably at best only half memories. We bring past incidents to mind, but the entire tone of the memory is often based on and colored by our present state of mind. A whole memory takes place when we try to recall exactly how our minds worked, how we felt, our consciousness, attitudes, problems, and struggles —in short, what our world looked like when we were six, twelve, sixteen, twenty, and so forth. This is not an easy exercise, but even an attempt at it will bring one a sense of ceaseless transformation of the human soul—a transformation, an unfolding that usually escapes our notice. Ho hum, we say, and begin another day.

One of the most important things I ever did in my adult

life was to journey back to my earliest memories. I returned to Scituate, Massachusetts, which is a small seacoast town. I walked the paths, the beaches and spent time in those places which had so impacted my life; the homes I lived in, the Church which was such a special place for me, the schools where I studied, the places I worked in, and those areas where I played and had fun. I tried to put myself back in time and to recall how the world looked to me then. Not for the purpose of judging my view now against my earlier views or for any judgmental purpose at all—just simply to feel and sense my own journey.

This experience was a very moving one, and I felt once again the pains and joys of being a human person on a journey. It was indeed a discovery that I had lost many qualities that I had had as a young person. Qualities such as spontaneity, trust, hope, love, openness, and others that I once knew and took for granted were, for the most part, no longer part of me. Many of those qualities were identified as "childlike," and we were continually reminded that they had "to go," in favor of growing more fully into the wisdom of the world. And so, like many others, I began to lose my uniqueness and began the process of trying to conform to the expectations of others and became absorbed into the values of my culture, which, as I later discovered, had little, if anything, to do with the Good News of Christ. The poet William Wordsworth, in one of his poems, speaks of the prison bars and the darkness that descends upon the heart and eyes as childhood wonder fades.

The past, of course, cannot be recaptured. When I speak about exercising memory, it is not in order to live in the past but to help invite wonder into the present. This, of course, is what Jesus meant when he asked each of us to become as little children, which he states is the way we enter the Kingdom. Somehow the sense of wonder over the fact of our own changing lives and relationships must be renewed.

Another important aspect of seeing life in terms of a journey is that it saves us from what scholars call literalism. Literalism is commonly expressed in phrases such as "Life is nothing but . . . ," "That's all there is," "What you see is what you get." Such views are unable to perceive things symbolically, unable to see that above and beyond one's little life, yet intimately connected to it there is a cosmic drama going on—the drama of creation, transformation, and redemption. The mythical traditions of all lands and times tell the story of the individual on his/her journey, one seeking a new life or treasure of some sort who, therefore, must struggle against the forces of darkness in order to achieve liberation, the pearl of great price, a sacred paradise.

Each one of us plays the central role in this drama. For the drama is at once yours and yet touches everyone, individual and yet cosmic at the same time. Jesus knew this very well and, by responding to the deeper currents of His individual life, the transcendent, He was able to bring about a way of redemption for all people. We must remember that at least until Jesus left home and began a life made solely of teaching and preaching, He did live a normal humdrum life on the surface. Like each of us, Jesus woke up each morning and faced the ordinary and demanding things that constitute daily life. The old abbot used to say that we do holy things all day long and never become holy—a preoccupation with external things that do not flow from within one's heart. For Christ these daily realities were revelations of His Father's workings, and He began the journey, the adventure that encompassed

His whole life and set it on another plane of meaning. In other words, the visible world, the ups and downs of daily life were for Jesus of Nazareth simply clues and invitations to the invisible world of His Father, the reality of which He declared to be of far greater value than the reality we usually ascribe to our mundane existence.

Is such a vision of the journey, of the symbolic value of our lives, even approximately possible for each of us? I once heard the philosopher Allen Watts make a very bold and rather rude statement, and yet it contained a great deal of truth. He said that Jesus Christ stands in His glory pointing the Way, but instead of going that way most of us have chosen to suck his finger. Watts was saying that most of us pay homage to a set of teachings and to an image, giving lip service to externals. But the real Christian way is to internalize the message of Christ, so that we live it out in our own journey. Cardinal John Henry Newman said the same things as Allen Watts, but less audaciously, when he said that the crucial issue concerning faith is whether you give merely a notional assent or a real assent. By notional assent Newman means a "yes" spoken with your head but not with your whole being. We say "yes" to Jesus, but then refuse to follow or even try to understand the way He pointed out. Real assent is operational, it is a true yes, because we try to live out our expressed faith in our daily life.

Faith opens our lives as journeys, as adventures into the reality of the Kingdom that is within us and all around us, for which the visible world and all its realities—our bodies, food, occupations, trials, and our joys—are meant to be symbols and clues. Your journey is not just a wandering, but rather it is a pilgrimage toward a goal, a search. Yet, it is a curious kind of goal, a strange kind of searching, for it is only in the journeying and the searching, not in the finding, the ending, that we actually discover and find the true meaning. Jesus tells us that the treasure is buried in the field: the field is our lives. To find the treasure is to unearth the ongoing source of meaning and richness which Faith give us the power to do.

One of the major obstacles to this searching is human inertia, complacency. Why should I search? Things are going fine. I'm basically satisfied. To tell the truth, the religious wisdom of our heritage can say little to a person who poses this sort of question. Religious teachings make their mature entry, and the pilgrimage begins in earnest only when you sense that something has been lost or that you are lost and that you need to find something, or to be found. Without a sense of suffering or imperfection, a sense that life is something hollow or out of joint, all exhortations to the search will fall on deaf ears. The seeds of the Kingdom will fall on fallow ground. But if you sense that behind the ebb and flow of our energies and interests, behind the little joys and pains there lies a more cosmic drama, then perhaps you have the ears to hear the Jesus so often mentioned.

Not to search is to be content with easy answers, to close off mystery, to be content with the division of work and leisure in your life, and to say "no" to change and to the invitation of Christ to set out on a journey. The spiritual journey is not another "job" to be added to your life. This compartmentalized view of spirituality is one of the misunderstandings of our day. No, the spiritual journey in its essential generosity addresses and touches every aspect of life. The secret of its power to do so lies in the fact that it is not another sort of duty, but rather an attitude, a mode of being which underlies all duties, which one carries through all the moments of one's day. This developing and strengthening attitude begins to transform the quality of our lives and to open our eyes to that often unseen reality, the love of God.

When we discuss such issues we are posing questions about a commitment to a way of life, an orientation, a direction. One can never stop asking the question, and yet each time you pose the question it is asked in an either/or way—you ask for a yes or a no. You can commit yourself or refuse to do so. Theologians call this crossroad "fundamental option," because it is a choice that deals with the orientations of one's life. When you avoid these questions about belief you will flounder and drift in life. This is the ground, the area of decision from which the Christian is able to grow and develop. All through the New Testament the Christian is being asked to choose, to make a radical decision, a fundamental option, a choice to enter a relational process of change and development. Christ made it very clear that you had to choose to be a follower, and he pointed this out when He said: "Anyone who wants to save his life will lose it; but anyone who loses his life for my sake, and for the sake of the gospel, will save it" (Mk 8:35); ". . . take up his cross and follow me" (Mk 8:34); "Enter by the narrow gate, since the road that leads to destruction is wide and spacious, and many take it; but it is a narrow gate and a hard road that leads to life, and only a few find it" (Mt 7:13–14); "Set your hearts on his kingdom first, and on God's saving justice, and all these other things will be given you as well" (Mt 6:33). Fundamental option, then, is that choice which deals with the totality of one's existence, its meaning and its direction—it brings into play the core of a person, the conscious and the unconscious, the rational and irrational, and all the facets of one's being.

The decision to follow Christ must be radical, a total commitment! In saying "yes" to His invitation to come and follow Him, each of us sets out on an exciting adventure. As I look back on my own journey, I can say it transcends all the dreams I had as a young boy when I first heard His invitation and said "yes."

I grew up in a basically loving family. My parents at times were at odds and yet they paid the price of their "yes" to one another and to Christ—they attempted to live out their commitment. In that Christian family setting I first heard the invitation of Christ. The invitation was received as an opportunity to set out on a great adventure which, in no small way, was because of my Irish heritage. Every Irishman is an adventurer. I was raised in a small town and my home overlooked the ocean. The sea has been an important part of my journey. I learned to sail early in life and I began to think of my life, my following Christ, as a great adventure . . . I would one day sail across the ocean and bring the Good News to all the world. My mother would often take me to the jetty, which protected the entrance to the harbor, and would teach me to sit still and listen to God in the wind, in the sea, in life. She would say, "Be quiet and He will speak to you."

He did speak to me, and for a long time in my young adult life, I tried my best to run from Him. I no longer went to the jetty to sit and listen—I did not want to hear Him in the wind and the sea . . . I didn't want to hear him at all because it was too painful. He seemed to ask for too much! After many years of struggling to find direction, and having left the seminary to pursue my goal of marriage and family, I found myself sitting in the darkness of the local church, a place which was very special in my life. The lights went on in the sanctuary and the priest appeared with two young people, one of whom was a childhood friend. They proceeded to go through the rehearsal for their marriage. In the dark corner of the church where

I was sitting, I once again heard His call, "Will you come and follow me?" This time I knew with certitude that He was calling me to the priesthood or religious life—a vocation I did not want. I left the church and walked the beach, and finally found myself sitting at the base of the light which warned the boats where the jetty was as they entered the harbor, and there again I said "yes."

I broke off the relationship with the girl I had fallen in love with while I was in the seminary, and continued my studies in order to complete my undergraduate work. I graduated from college and began my graduate studies. My "yes" began to fade and I could not seem to run fast enough, and He pursued me wherever I went. While working in New York as a social worker, I sought out a spiritual director in an effort to resolve my confusion.

In the course of spiritual direction, I again heard His invitation and went to St. Joseph's Abbey to make a retreat and to resolve the question that was haunting me. During that retreat, it became obvious to me beyond any possible doubt that He was calling me to religious life and that I was free to make a choice—it was an either/or decision. I said "yes." I entered a Trappist monastery. I felt it was the total gift of myself to Him. I wanted to let go of everything and give my whole being to Him. I felt that by leaving the world, my family, and loved ones, and entering a life of prayer and discipline, my act would be a sign of my surrender to Him.

The early days of my monastic life were most difficult. In those days they shaved your hair off, and I literally lived from one haircut to another, thinking that if I could just hang on and get the haircut, I wouldn't leave with a bald head. Slowly I began to love the simplicity of the life and the community. The years passed quickly and I grew more and more to love the life, and I found a deep inner peace and joy. It all changed when I became sick and my illness was believed to be incompatible with the austerity of the Trappist life. I was told that I would have to leave behind the life I had grown to love so much . . . I would have to let go!

Why must I leave and return to the world that I had left? In the midst of my anguish I heard a voice say, "Why did you become a Trappist?" I answered, "Because I wanted to give you everything." "Did you give me everything?" "Yes, what else do I have? I left my family, my loved ones, the world . . . everything!" "If you left everything, then why won't you let go and come follow me?" I cried for a long time because it was the first time that I had realized that I had been following my way and that I was still hanging on to my way—my response to His invitation. I finally said *"Fiat"* (So be it), you can have it all. At that moment my whole being filled with a great inner peace and joy which I shall never forget. Once again in my journey He had spoken to me in and through events and people and gave me the help I needed to "listen" and to be able to say *"Yes."* This time, I let go and set out to never again know where I was going. I wanted only to be a true pilgrim on a journey, totally dependent upon Christ.

Since that dramatic moment, my life has been an adventure, and He has taken me where I would never have gone on my own. Each of us sets out and must continually try to listen and then respond with our gift, our "yes." Our security must be found only in trusting Him with all that we are and have, being certain that He will never fail us.

The journey that each of us is on, our pilgrimage, is described in various ways by the mystics. St. John Climacus describes the spiritual journey in terms of climbing a ladder. St. Teresa of Ávila uses various images:

her seven mansions, the various ways of watering the garden, and so forth. The purgative, illuminative, and contemplative are another way of seeing the journey. The author of *The Cloud of Unknowing,* a fourteenth-century English mystic, states that the Christian life, the journey, "seems to progress through four ascending phases of growth, which I call the Common, the Special, the Singular, and the Perfect."[1] For him these phases are descriptive of an ever-deepening life of friendship with the Lord. Still others describe it in terms of those who are beginners, the advanced, and the perfect. From the early Church into our own times various authors, in attempting to describe growth in the spiritual life, have looked on the journey as a challenge of passage from our first "yes," to the invitation of Christ to follow Him and begin that process, to a series of other affirmations of our desire to follow Him. The mystics point out that there are obstacles, and that many begin the journey and never finish. They stop on the way and become comfortable, secure, or entangled in compensations which prevent them from hearing the Master—they are unwilling to pay the price of their "yes," and here is where they begin to drift and loose their sense of direction. Yet, they also affirm that the Lord never gives up, and even though we fail in our commitment to follow Him, He continually reaches out to reinvite us to follow Him and to find meaning and peace on our journey.

With the emerging schools of psychology and social sciences during the post–World War II era, followed by extensive research into our own time, we have available today a vast amount of material dealing with growth and development of the human person. In their attempt to understand the various passages that we go through they, like the mystics, describe them in ways that are quite similar. When you compare the writings of the mystics and spiritual authors of former times with the social scientists of today, you can see similarities and you become aware that the mystics and saints were indeed grounded in the fundamental principles concerning growth. Yet, they did not have available the enormous amount of information that we have today, and thus it becomes essential for us to examine the insights of psychologists and social scientists in order to have a more profound understanding of the stages of growth. They not only describe various passages, but they place before us the challenges that we face if we choose to continue to be open to the process of growth.

The Center for Human Development has made extensive use of various psychological tools to both facilitate self-knowledge and indicate the challenges that participants in our various programs face, if they wish to say yes to growing into the fullness of their uniqueness. I stress that they are tools which can help us, and it would indeed be a terrible mistake to pay no attention to their findings. We have made use of the theory set forth by Jane Loevinger, which offers us one way of looking at the challenges that we face if we wish to grow and continue our journey. After her consideration of those stages dealing with childhood development, she goes on to describe the stage where many people seem to adjust to and remain—the role-conformity stage. She describes this stage and the transitions to higher stages as follows:

> More people have recognized this [conformity] stage than any other. Here the child identifies himself with authority; his parents at first, later other adults, then his peers. This is the period of greatest cognitive simplicity. There is a right way and a wrong way, and it is the same for everyone all the time, or for broad

classes of people . . . What is conventional and socially approved is right . . . rules are accepted because they are socially accepted . . . Disapproval becomes a potent sanction. There is high value for friendliness and social niceness. Cognitive preoccupations are appearance, material things, reputation, and social acceptance . . . People and one's own self are perceived in terms of social group classifications. Individual differences are scarcely perceived. The way things or people are and the way they ought to be are not sharply separated . . . People in the conformist stage constitute either a majority or a large minority in almost any social group.

The transition between the conformist and the conscientious stages is marked by heightened consciousness of self and of inner feelings. A related aspect of the transition is perception of multiple possibilities in situations. Rules are seen to have exceptions or to hold only in certain contingencies. Inner states and individual differences are described in vivid and differentiated ways. One feels guilty not primarily when one has broken a rule, but when one has hurt another person. Motives and consequences are more important than rules per se. Long-term goals and ideals are characteristic: "ought" is clearly different from "is." The individual is aware of choices; he strives for goals, he is concerned with living up to ideals and improving himself. The moral imperative remains, but it is no longer just a matter of doing right and avoiding wrong. There are questions of priorities and appropriateness . . . Achievement is important, and it is measured by one's own inner standards rather than being primarily a matter of competition or social approval.

The transition from the conscientious to the autonomous stage is marked by a heightened sense of individuality and a concern for emotional independence. The problem of dependence-independence is recurrent throughout ego development. What characterizes this? The autonomous stage is so named partly because one recognizes other people's need for autonomy, partly because it is marked by some freeing sense of responsibility during the conscientious stage. Moral dichotomies are no longer characteristic. They are replaced by a feeling for the complexity and multifaceted character of real people and real situations. There is a deepened respect for other people and their need to find their own mistakes . . . We do not believe that inner conflict is more characteristic of the autonomous stage than of lower stages. Rather, the autonomous person has the courage to acknowledge, to cope with conflict rather than blotting it out or projecting it onto the environment. The autonomous person is concerned with social problems beyond his own immediate experience. He tries to be realistic about himself and others.

In most social groups one will find no more than perhaps 1%, and usually fewer, at our highest or integrated level . . . only a few individuals reach the stage of transcending conflict and reconciling polarities that we call the integrated stage.

There is a temptation to see the successive stage of ego development as problems to be solved and to assume that the best-adjusted people are those at the highest stages . . . Probably those who remain below the conformist level beyond childhood can be called maladjusted . . . Some self-protective opportunistic persons, on the other hand, become very successful . . . Certainly it is a conformist's world, and many conformists are very happy with it, though they are not all immune to mental illness. Probably to be faithful to the realities of the case, one should see the sequence as one of coping with increasingly deeper problems rather than as the successful negotiation of solutions.[2]

As Loevinger points out, most people progress to the role-conformity stage, and this is confirmed by other research and is an accepted fact, and rest there. This conformity stage indicates that for many the meaning of life is outside themselves—their self-concept and identity is measured through meeting external standards which drives them more and more to achieve self-acceptance and a positive self-regard. Their search is in vain. Our growth in this fundamental area takes place primarily in and through the influence of people capable of loving us, as we are. This, as we shall see later, is always a taste of His unconditional love, which alone frees us from the slavery of conformity and expectations of others. The Center during the past fifteen years has found very few priests and religious at this stage, which indicates that they are in a critical position in their call to ministry to facilitate and promote the growth of people.

The transition between conformist and the conscientious stages opens one to choices and one becomes aware that life is not black and white. Lower-stage people will hold rigidly to rules and laws, as though they contain the ultimate meaning, and are unable to transcend them in particular situations. In the old theology, the Church always taught that every rule, every law in the Church had to be based and grounded in one law, the commandment of *love!* Therefore, in given situations one could actually break a given rule or law in order to fulfill the law of love —this was using *epekia.* It was in the books, but most of us

were scared to death to use it and because we were unable to assume responsibility for this, or we lacked the
inner freedom, we often fulfilled the obligations of a law
and failed in *charity!* I recall a good example of this from
my own family background, when one time several of my
brothers were very sick and my mother missed Mass on a
Sunday in order to care for them. My father was quite
concerned that she mention this to the priest in confession and my mother rejected this and tried to explain to
him that she had an obligation to take care of the kids and
had no guilt feelings or need to confess something which
was done because of the demands of her state of life and
the commandment of love. Many of us probably recall
times when we violated some particular law and, lacking
the inner freedom, felt guilty even though we knew that
the law was subservient to charity. In this transitional
stage, we are really looking at a growing realization and
acceptance of the fact that we need one another and are
dependent from birth to death. In other words, we grow
in and through community—the community of our
friends, family, and loved ones. Lower-stage people fail to
grasp this fundamental reality and strive for independence and to make it on their own—they don't need anyone!

The autonomous stage describes individuals who have
been able to negotiate the challenges of the journey and
have grown into an acceptance of who they are—
wounded pilgrims on a journey. They now know and have
tasted the unconditional love of the Father . . . they are
free! Until one reaches this stage, true inner freedom is
rarely experienced, and yet Christ calls us to be "free."
Hence, it is imperative for each of us not to succumb to
the norms of the given cultures and various structures
that we live under, but to continually strive to follow

Christ and be willing to pay the price of our commitment. He alone is the Way, the Truth, and the Life, and anyone or anything that tries to sidetrack us from Him must be rejected, regardless of the price.

Each of us moves from stage to stage; we do grow from infancy, to childhood, to young adulthood, to adulthood. This is certainly true of physical development and even though, at times, we find comfort in a given stage of internal growth, we might even get stuck, we must never fail to realize that we can once again begin to follow Him. He continually reaches out to each of us and offers us opportunities to respond. We need to listen to His invitation, an invitation that almost always comes to us via events, people, and circumstances, and yet behind all of these He reaches out to us and beckons us to once again put our trust in Him. We need only dare to give up our false security, controls, and certitudes and once again embrace a life of faith, trust, love, prayer, and discipline. It is indeed a risky task to follow Him and to put all of our confidence in Him, but it is the only way: this is the path to our human destiny.

The above material indicates, and has certainly been confirmed over and over again in the work of the Center, that one of the major challenges that the Church must face in our time is that of "formation." There is a crying need for direction, guidance, and even structures that are capable of assisting members of the Church as they face the challenge of Christ to grow. In the post–Vatican II Church there were priests and religious who threw out much of what we had from the past and treated it as irrelevant, and in the midst of the vacuum that was created we fled to the behavioral sciences for solutions. We took from these sciences bits of information and failed, in my estimation, to integrate these new insights with our rich spiritual heritage. Rules and laws have their place in formation—structures are essential, if you want to promote growth. The reward and punishment stages of growth are part and parcel of growth, just as a child must first be an infant. The task that we must face is ministering to individuals, communities, whether they be religious, priests, parishes. Wherever we find the people of God, we must assist them in continuing their journey, their pilgrimage to the Father. The integration of our mystical tradition with the knowledge that is available to us today concerning growth and development is an urgent need. We can no longer throw up our hands and cry for a return to the past models of formation or, on the other hand, reject the past and try to build new models without reference to our history. This is an example of where it is not an either/or, but rather it must be both/and!

The mystics had a marvelous way of bringing the most seemingly complicated issues into a focus, a clarity, and above all in a simple way. The author of *The Cloud of Unknowing* lacked the insights of modern psychologists concerning growth, and yet in his simple way he places it before us in a beautiful way which anyone can grasp.

> For out of all his flock he has lovingly chosen you to be one of his special friends. He has led you to sweet meadows and nourished you with his love, strengthening you to press on so as to take possession of your heritage in his kingdom.

> I urge you, then, pursue your course relentlessly. Attend to tomorrow and let yesterday be. Never mind what you have gained so far. Instead reach out to what lies ahead. If you wish to keep growing you must nourish in your heart the lively longing for God. Though

this loving desire is certainly God's gift, it is up to you
to nurture it. But mark this, God is a jealous lover. He is
at work in your spirit and will tolerate no meddlers.
The only other one He needs is you.[3]

God needs you to say yes to your own unique journey, a
journey that will never again be duplicated. There is only
one you, and your pilgrimage was meant to be an exciting,
challenging adventure. How do you begin to find the path
again, or to start off on this journey, this response to
Christ's invitation to follow Him? In the following chapters, we will explore and surface our rich heritage. We will
look not only at the principles and insights of the mystics
and saints, but also at the knowledge we've gained from
other sources concerning growth and development.

"WILL YOU COME FOLLOW ME?"

"THE WINDS OF GOD'S GRACE ARE ALWAYS BLOWING, BUT WE MUST MAKE AN EFFORT TO RAISE OUR SAILS."

REFLECTIONS

1. Identify when you first were conscious of responding
   to Christ's invitation to follow Him. Were there other
   moments, crossroads, where you again experienced
   His call? What was the setting in which you made your
   decision? How did you feel?

2. List the significant events in your journey. What was
   the message you took from those events? What do you
   think God might have been trying to tell you?

3. Identify three viewpoints, views that have meant
   something to you. Have you changed through insights

that you've been given through Scripture, prayer, Vatican II, or other vehicles? How did you feel at the time of the change? How did you handle the change?

SUGGESTED READINGS

1. Walter J. Burghardt. *Seasons That Laugh or Weep: Musings on the Human Journey.* Paulist Press, 1983.

2. Evelyn and James Whitehead. *Christian Life Patterns.* Doubleday, 1979.

3. James W. Fowler. *Becoming Adult, Becoming Christian: Adult Development and Christian Faith.* Harper & Row, 1984.

4. Gustavo Gutiérrez. *We Drink from Our Own Wells: The Spiritual Journey of a People.* Translated by Matthew J. O'Connell. Orbis Books, 1984.

CHAPTER II

TWO THINGS NECESSARY FOR THE JOURNEY

There seems to be nothing that is so vital to each of us as that which has to do with ourselves, the meaning of our lives, our relationships with everyone and everything. History indicates that this concern has also been one of the past, and each of us stands in the unfolding process of this history. The present understanding of the meaning of life is due in no small part to the men and women of the past. The development that has taken place in the past number of years, and in which we find ourselves today somewhat strained trying to keep abreast of, has changed many of our views. With this process of an ever-deepening understanding of man/woman, the world, and life itself, we have become more aware of the needs of each person, one's need to find the meaning of one's life, to unify one's activities, to integrate one's life.

Christian spirituality may be spoken of in terms of our response to God revealing Himself from moment to moment. It is the life of each unique person facing his/her God, participating in the life of God, the spirit of each person listening to the Spirit of God. It includes relationships, and embraces one's whole life—every aspect of human living. Spirituality thus is unique with each person, and although there are common traits, there are no duplications. We can, therefore, speak of a spirituality of a given period of time, and it is important to trace the insights of others into the Christian message from former times. Once we locate the basic themes, we must then transfer them into our own present day in the light of development. Only when we have accomplished this task are we able to speak to those of our time with a freshness that makes the message of Christ relevant and dynamic.

One of the great spiritual classics, *The Cloud of Unknowing,* has a popularity today which is not too difficult to understand in relationship to the spiritual hunger that is all around us. The author has never been identified, and it is evident that he wished to remain anonymous. Historians conclude that he wrote the book in the late fourteenth century. William Johnston in his introduction to his edition of the work states:

> He belongs to a century made famous in the annals of spirituality by the names of Richard Rolle, Juliana of Norwich, and Walter Hilton in England; by Meister Eckhard, John Tauler, and Henry Suso in Germany; by Jan van Ruysbroeck in Flanders; by Jacopone da Todi and Catherine of Siena in Italy. This is an age associated with the names of Angela de Foligno and Thomas a Kempis. It is an age when, in spite of troubles and rumbling presages of a coming storm, Europe was deeply religious: faith penetrated to the very hearts of the people and influenced not only their art, music, and literature, but every aspect of their lives. Merry England was saturated with a religious faith that breaks forth in *Piers Plowman* and the *Canterbury Tales.* Chaucer may laugh good-humoredly at the foi-

bles of nuns and friars, but he accepted the established religion with an unquestioning mind. Such was the society in which the author of *The Cloud* lived and wrote: both he and his public took for granted a Church, a faith, and a sacramental life that are no longer accepted without question by many readers today.

He was, then, a thoroughgoing medieval, steeped in the spirit of his time and imbued with its tradition. So many of his words, phrases, and ideas are also found in *The Imitation of Christ,* in the De Adhaerendo Deo, in the writings of the Rhineland mystics, and in the other devotional treatises of the time that one immediately sees him as part of a great current of medieval spirituality.[1]

Our rich spiritual heritage flows from one great mystic to another, and Johnston points out the similarity of the unknown English mystic with St. John of the Cross, who wrote about the spiritual journey two centuries later. Johnston states: "So it is the great stream of a common tradition that has formed the minds of these two great men, both being part of a mystical current that has flowed through Christian culture, breaking down the barriers of space and time separating fourteenth century England and sixteenth century Spain; nor have its surging waves lost their power in the twentieth century."[2]

I agree with Johnston's conclusion that *The Cloud of Unknowing* does indeed have a relevancy to us today. The title of this chapter is "Two Things Necessary for the Journey." The author of *The Cloud of Unknowing* tells us that "whoever acquires these two habits of mind and manner needs no others, for he will possess everything."[3]

These two virtues that he is referring to are *humility and brotherly love*. Therefore, all we need to acquire in order for us to set out on our journey in following Christ and to be successful is humility and love of one another. I should point out that many of the earlier writers used masculine terms, which for them and in their own times embraced women. Thus it would be wrong to judge them in the light of our present sensitivity to language, and I can only ask you to embrace the meaning.

Many years ago, I read a book that had a profound impact on me. It was *Perceiving, Behaving, and Becoming,* by Dr. Arthur Coombs. The thrust of his work was that your perceptional viewpoint determines your behavior and the possibility of becoming. In other words, your behavior flows directly from the way you look at things— your perception! It thus becomes critical for each of us to be in touch with our viewpoints, many of which were put into us at a young age, and unless we have undergone a conversion they are still there, determining our behavior and effecting the possibility of growth. For instance, you have a view, a perception concerning humility. When I was young my perception of the virtue of humility was to "put yourself down" and not to accept compliments. I would reject compliments by remarks like "Well, it was really nothing" or "I could have done much better." Even when I read some spiritual authors, they would confirm this attitude. Once I read a spiritual book and the "holy person" described himself as nothing but dung! Well, I said to myself, "If he feels that about himself, then I must be a pile of dung!"

It is very important for you to take a few moments and reflect on your viewpoint concerning humility. What does it mean to you? Where did you get that understanding? On your journey have you changed your perception of this virtue? If so, can you recall what brought that about? Reflecting on these questions will enable you to get in touch with yourself at this moment of your journey. As we examine the view of the author of *The Cloud*, perhaps it will call you from your present understanding and open you up to a new way of perceiving it.

The English mystic tells us that humility may be viewed as imperfect and perfect—there are two sides to the coin. He describes these two viewpoints when he says, "A man is humble when he stands in the truth with a knowledge and appreciation for himself as he really is. And actually, anyone who saw and experienced himself as he really and truly is would have no difficulty being humble, for two things would become very clear to him."[4] The first thing that he refers to is what he calls imperfect humility, and the second is perfect humility. It is essential that each of us is grounded and in touch with both sides of the coin, otherwise our journey will become more and more difficult. He goes on to say:

> In the first place, he would see clearly the degradation, misery, and weakness of the human condition resulting from original sin. From these effects of original sin man will never be entirely free in this life, no matter how holy he becomes.
>
> In the second place, he would recognize the transcendent goodness of God as he is in himself and his overflowing, superabundant love for man. Before such goodness and love nature trembles, sages stammer like fools, and the saints and angels are blinded with glory. So overwhelming is this revelation of God's nature that if his power did not sustain them, I dare not think what might happen.[5]

Imperfect humility, then, is coming to know ourselves, especially in our woundedness, which is a direct result of original sin—a "given." He makes it very clear that there is no escape from this woundedness—"no matter how holy we become!" Other mystics describe this knowledge as being painful and difficult to accept—we are indeed wounded pilgrims on a journey to the Father. The author of *The Cloud* makes his point in a vivid and descriptive way when he says, "Fast as much as you like, watch far into the night, rise long before dawn, discipline your body, and if it were permitted—which it is not—put out your eyes, tear out your tongue, plug up your ears and nose, and cut off all your limbs: yes chastise your body with every discipline and you would still gain nothing. The desire and tendency toward sin would remain in your heart."[6] Later on, he adds to this by telling us that "Experience will teach you that in this life there is no absolute security or lasting peace. But never give up and do not become overly anxious about falling."[7]

In New England the clam-diggers would put it in another language, and in my hometown they would say: "Look, you were born all screwed-up and you'll be screwed-up until the day you die—so relax!" But they, like the mystics, would reaffirm the necessity to *never give up, never quit!* In our society we do a great job of helping one another to be in touch with our woundedness, imperfect humility. In fact, I would give you odds that at this very moment if you have any doubts concerning the fact that you are not perfect, then put the book down. I'm certain that if there is someone with you, that person will be delighted to help you progress in this area of self-knowledge. It is, as they say, a sure bet!

The other side of the coin of humility, perfect humility, is much more difficult to discover—it is in coming to know and taste the unconditional love of God! In the twelfth century St. Bernard of Clairvaux wrote the great classic on the Four Degrees of the Love of God, which we will look at more closely in a later chapter. It suffices for now to place before you his first degree, which might very well surprise you. He states that the beginning point of the love of God is love of self, which is nothing other than the internalization of the Good News. In the Good News, Christ reveals to each of us an incredible story concerning His love and the Father's love for each of us, just as we are. Let me place before you some questions which flow from the Good News, and from our heritage, and I ask you to reflect on them, then give your answer.

Do you believe in God?

Do you believe that Christ became man in order to communicate the unconditional love of the Father?

Do you believe that Christ took upon Himself all your faults and sins, died for you so that you could have life?

Do you believe that you were created in the likeness of God?

Do you believe that God has given you the power to love, to forgive, and to heal?

I could add many other questions to the above, and I suggest that you might find it fruitful to add some other questions which surface from your own recollection of reading the Good News. When I ask these questions, I've found that most people will respond by saying yes to each of the questions—they believe! But, having said yes with their heads, they in actual fact believe in their hearts to be worthless pieces of junk! Hence, St. Bernard would say you have flunked the course! And sad to say, you have

nowhere to go on the journey until you come to internalize the message, the Christ event in your life. Each of us
must come to know that we are indeed beautiful, lovable
persons and that God loves us at this moment, accepts us
as we are . . . too good to be true, but true!

When I was a young monk and first began to be exposed
to the writings of the author of *The Cloud*, St. Bernard,
and many others, I was actually astounded in what they
had to say about life, about following Christ. For instance,
no one had ever told me that the first challenge I faced
was in coming to accept and to love myself. I recall reading a letter from a monk to St. Bernard in which he pro-
fessed how much he loved Bernard and God. Bernard
wrote back and told him that it was impossible for him to
love him, let alone God, since he had not come to love
himself. At the time, I found this to be rather earthshak-
ing, and for me, it began a process of reviewing my formation and opening myself to the challenge of growth.

There is a favorite spot of mine in the monastery where
I used to go to ponder things and to pray. My spot was a
well on top of the hill, which gave me a view looking
across the fields, the hills, and the monastery. One day I
had gone there to reflect on all the above, and as I sat
there I became aware that whenever anyone had something good to say to me I would immediately brush it aside
with some comment like, "Oh well, I could have done
much better" or "If you really knew me you wouldn't say
that." As I reflected on it, I became acutely aware that the
good things that were said to me concerning myself were
rejected and the remarks about my faults and weaknesses
I, as it were, drank in without even a question. I asked
myself, "How did this ever happen?"

The answer came to me in a very humorous way. My
attention became focused on an old cow barn, where I

had many times shoveled the manure from the cow stalls to the end of the barn, and then opened a trapdoor so the manure could fall into the manure spreader. Out of nowhere, the lights went on and I exclaimed, "My God! I have spent my whole life under that trapdoor. No wonder I now have a smelly self-image!"

I found myself drifting back through my journey and recalling that in growing up in the "Harbor Irish" section of the town, I realized that there had been a definite effort to make sure that you would never become proud, since no one wanted you to go to Hell. Thus, they all seemed to participate, in varying degrees, in assisting me to be grounded in what the author of *The Cloud* calls imperfect humility. My father felt that he had a responsibility to help shape me up, so that whatever I was doing would be done with perfection, and thus he was good at opening the trapdoor on me.

One day I found myself in the Church kneeling before the statue of the Blessed Mother saying the Memorare, and as I was leaving I felt good about myself and said: "Well, the Blessed Mother loves me and Mom loves me most of the time, so I'm not so bad!" But on my way home, walking down the main street of the harbor, I ran into one of my brothers, who informed me that I was in trouble with Mom.

When I went off to school, I could never seem to draw correctly and my Palmer penmanship left much to be desired. So often I found myself staying after school and then having a long walk home, because I missed the regular school bus. When I reached the third year of high school, everyone agreed I had no future in education, having flunked so many subjects, not to mention the number of times I had been expelled, so I was sworn into the U.S. Navy on my seventeenth birthday.

Strange as it might seem to some, it was in the Navy that I began to see myself in a different light. I was accepted into the submarine service and then discovered that I was in the top 5 percent, which meant that I had an above-average IQ and also had to be psychologically balanced. I remember the day one of my abbots (there have been four since I entered) said to me that the monastery was something like being in the submarine service. I replied that there was one big difference—we were carefully chosen for the submarine service. I left the Navy because I felt the pull to give my life to God in the priesthood. I entered and left the seminary twice, finally convinced that I didn't have a vocation. I graduated from St. Anselm's College, where I had done well academically and had been deeply touched by the monks—their care, concern, and encouragement made a lasting impression on me. I continued my studies in graduate school, but never completed my degree in social work. I left the field of social work to enter the monastery. By this time my self-image had changed, and I was beginning to accept myself and to discover that I was a lovable human person.

When I entered the monastery, I felt that in such a loving community I would no longer experience the trapdoor. However, I discovered that in and through the Chapter of Faults the trapdoor was open several times each week, but now it was in the form of fraternal correction—rooted in love and the desire to assist me in my growth! Call it by any name, the effect was that the manure was continually coming down on my head. Well, as I sat there on the well, I found myself saying, "Well, this is just me, no one else would ever have had this happen to them!"

When I came out of the monastery and went to Catholic University, I began to work with priests and I discovered that they were experts on opening the trapdoor on one another. All you had to do was walk into a room of priests and the trapdoor would open on you, usually in the form of a joke, but the effect was the same—the manure had fallen on you! In fact, in order to control how much manure would fall on you, you would open the trapdoor yourself, so that at least you could control how much manure was going to fall on your head. I concluded that this must just be a trait of priests, but then I began to work with nuns and I discovered that the sisters too were very good at opening the trapdoor; however, they at least did it with a smile. I then felt that this was probably just a part of religious life, but then in working with laypeople I found that they too were excellent and skilled at opening the trapdoor. I, therefore, have concluded from my experiences that most of us have spent at least some time under the trapdoor. We need to shut the trapdoor, nail it down . . . forever!

The Chapter of Faults is gone, along with many of the old ways that we opened the trapdoor on one another. However, there are new ways, and when someone approaches you and says "I'd like to give you some feedback" or "I'd like to share with you my feelings," you can be sure, most of the time, the trapdoor is about to open on you. So be careful!

After I completed my doctorate, I accepted an appointment to the faculty of the University of North Carolina at Charlotte, where I taught in the School of Human Development and Learning. It was there that I became interested in the movement called "Human Potential." At that time, research in this field indicated that most of us only operate on 8–16 percent of our potential. Needless to say, that is alarming, and as a result of this awareness, millions of research dollars were spent in exploring the causes and discovering ways to release this potential. One of the major blocks to the release of our potential is poor self-concept!

I found this interesting in the light of St. Bernard's treatment of the four stages of the love of God. St. Bernard, in the twelfth century without any research grant from the King of France, had discovered through reflection and prayer on the Scriptures that a positive self-concept was essential for the journey. St. Bernard certainly didn't have the depth of understanding that we have today concerning self-concept and self-image, but he did know that the internalization of the Good News of Christ had to bring about within each of us a positive self regard. Coming to this positive self-image is not an easy task; in fact, it is usually a slow process with plenty of ups and downs.

As I've reflected on this, I have come to believe that we have directed almost all of our energy in helping one another to be rooted in the necessary knowledge of imperfect humility. But, as the author of *The Cloud* points out, there is also perfect humility, and one must come to know and taste both imperfect and perfect humility in order to make the journey. In regard to perfect humility, the author of *The Cloud* says:

> The humility engendered by this experiential knowledge of God's goodness and love I call perfect, because it is an attitude which man will retain even in eternity. But the humility arising from a realistic grasp of the human condition I call imperfect, for not only will it pass away at death with its cause, but even in this life it will not always be operative. For sometimes people well advanced in the contemplative life will receive such grace from God that they will be suddenly

and completely taken out of themselves and neither remember nor care whether they are holy or sinful.

> . . . though they may lose all concern for their sinfulness or virtue, they do not lose the sense of God's immense love and goodness and therefore, they have perfect humility.[8]

One day when I was feeling down and discouraged, and thinking that I wasn't worth much—all I could seem to see was the negative side of things and my faults and weaknesses were like a tremendous weight around my neck—In that moment of despair I felt the presence of Christ in a very special way, saying to me, "Hey, wait a minute . . . I knew you in your mother's womb, my Father sent me to take your sins and faults to myself and to die on the cross in order to free you. I sent the Spirit to be with you. We dwell inside you and are with you all the time. I told you my mercy endures forever, my love is steadfast. I have the hairs of your head numbered, I know you by name . . ." and on and on until I finally broke down and cried, saying, "Why can't I really believe?"

Perhaps you've never had such an experience, but let me ask you to take a few moments, put the book down for a while, and reflect on your own journey, recalling the times that you've felt and maybe believed that you were worthless and hated the self you found.

Where are you now? Do you believe in your worth? Do you believe in the crazy, unconditional love that God has for you—a *given*, with no strings attached? What will it take to get you to believe in the Christ event?

"Come follow Me" is the invitation that you once heard and responded to and perhaps, like myself, there have been times on your journey when you turned off even your "hearing aids" and walked to the tune of another drummer. There is another way of looking at this invitation by turning it around into two other questions or invitations: "Will you be my friend? Will you love one another?"

My own views on friendship have been deeply influenced and shaped by the writings of St. Bernard and St. Aelred. In our own time the words of Pope Paul VI, especially in his encyclical *Paths of the Church*, have provided me with new thoughts and ways of looking at the life of friendship.

The whole message of Christ is one of love. Jesus spoke of only one commandment as specifically His: "This is my commandment: love one another, as I have loved you" (Jn 15–12). The parable of the King who will come at the end and reward all those who have lived lives of love indicated that love of one another is the love of God (Mt 25:31–46). St. John reminds us that "whoever does not love the brother whom he can see cannot love God whom he has not seen" (1 Jn 4:20). Karl Rahner, an eminent theologian of our own time reflecting upon the message of Christ, maintains that the love of God and man are ontologically the same. In loving my neighbor, in and by that very act, I love God, whether or not I advert to it consciously.[9]

The mystics continually remind us that God can speak to us in two ways: directly and indirectly. God can appear to you with a choir of angels and look at you, eyeball to eyeball, and, in the midst of that beautiful background of the angelic choirs singing, tell you that He loves you, as you are! On the other hand, He can transmit this same incredible message in and through the events of our lives, and primarily in and through the people He sends into our lives. I guess most of us would prefer that He would come down with a choir of angels and thus make it impossible for us to ever again doubt our beauty, but the normal way that we come to know His crazy love for us is in and through our friends, family, the community we live in, the Church. We will explore this life of friendship in a later chapter, but for now it suffices to say we must be more keenly aware of how we touch one another, especially those close to us.

Christ was not just an historical figure; He continues to live and He has chosen to live in us, to continue His life in and through each of us. You are, thus, reliving the paschal mystery in your own journey. You have been given the power to communicate the unconditional love of God and also the power to receive or reject the Christ event in your own life. If you choose to receive and to internalize the Good News, then you'll be on the road to an ever deeper positive self-concept and inner freedom—the freedom of the children of God! The question that is most important is, Where are you? Do you communicate the love within you? Are you open to receiving love from others?

A major turning point in my own journey took place at the time of my graduation from Catholic University. My father had decided to come to Washington for the graduation with some of the other members of my family. The graduation ceremonies were scheduled to take place outside, and since it was expected to be a very hot and humid day, I arranged it so he and the family could watch the ceremonies from within an air-conditioned building that gave them a great view of everything. My father decided that he wanted to stay outside, so he stood throughout the ceremonies under a tree by himself.

When the ceremony was finished I began to walk toward where my father was, feeling proud of the fact that I had earned a doctorate. I was wearing my academic robes

over my clerical suit, both signs of realities that were part
of my father's dream, if not also my mother's, for each of
their children. My father, I suppose like many Irish fathers, always had hoped that one of us would go on to the
priesthood and that we would all go on to higher education. Well, there I was embracing both aspects of his
dream, and the one most unlikely to have achieved them.
So, when I reached my father, I asked him, "Well, Dad,
did you ever think I'd make it?" He responded, "Oh, of
course, I knew you'd make it!" I was surprised, to say the
least (recalling the past), and said to him, "Really?" He
then said, "Well, to tell you the truth—it's a miracle!" The
trapdoor opened again and down came the manure. But
then the family joined us and we went off to celebrate the
"miracle."

I returned home with the family, and after a few days
my father invited me to walk with him along the beach.
As we were walking together I noticed that the tide was
out and there were people digging clams on the clam flats.
It brought back memories. I turned to my father and
asked him if he remembered the times when he would say
to me, "If you don't shape up, you'll be nothing but a
clam-digger!" Clam digging in those days was about the
lowest thing you could do; today it is a lucrative business.
He had no difficulty remembering that he often had said
that to me. I then went on to share with him how deeply
that had bothered me as a young boy growing up. It got to
me even more when he would say it to me in front of
Mom, and Mom never said anything, so I began to believe
that both of them felt that I couldn't do much else with
my life. Well, my father was shocked and said, "Well, look
at what you've done with your life—you're a priest, you
have a doctorate degree, you're going off to teach at a
major university, and your mother and I always knew that

you had the gifts and talents to do just about anything you wanted, but when you were young you didn't do a damn thing. You flunked your courses and were always fooling around. I had to motivate you, and thank God I did motivate you because if I hadn't, you'd be out there digging clams right now!"

I turned to my father and told him that it hadn't motivated me; on the contrary, it had led me to believe that I wasn't worth much and probably couldn't accomplish much. He turned to me and asked me if I knew that he and my mom both loved me no matter what happened? Without any hesitation, I responded by telling him, "No, Dad, I didn't know that." It was the second time I saw my father cry. The first time was when Mom died and here I again, after so many years, saw the tears rolling down the cheeks of this old man. With a broken voice he said "You dummy!" He finally took off his glasses and dried his eyes and asked me, "When did you ever come to us and we weren't there for all you kids?" I said, "You were always there for us." "Do you remember when you were young and I lost everything in the depression, did you kids ever go without anything, didn't you always have food, clothes, a place for you and for your friends?" "Yes, Dad, you both were there and it was obvious to all of us the sacrifices that you made for us." "Then, how come you didn't know that we loved you no matter what happened—whether you became a priest, doctor, or even a clam-digger . . . didn't you know we loved you no matter what would happen?"

It was a sad moment for me, when in truth I had to turn to this great man and say, "Dad, I never knew it because you and Mom never told me, never said it." He was taken back by this and said, "But we said it by doing all those things for you." I felt sad when I told him that I had never received the "incredible message," their unconditional love for me—the Good News had not penetrated my heart.

I asked my father if he would mind if I went along the beach alone out to the breakwater, at the entrance to the harbor. He went along the beach in the other direction, and I returned to one of my favorite spots as a young boy. When I reached the end of the jetty I sat there reflecting on all that had taken place between my father and me. I found myself looking out on the sea and saying, "Isn't this a crazy world—here this old man had all this love for his boy and the world told him not to tell me how much he loved me." I began to see that culture was the culprit and not the message of Christ. In fact, I'm convinced that many of us have sold ourselves to cultural values and have left behind the Good News!

There have been times when I've told that story and people would say to me it was my fault that I didn't get the message. They did tell you their love for you in and through deeds. We need to realize that we are all unique —what might get through to one doesn't necessarily get through to another. Those of you who have children know this to be very true—no two are alike. It seems to me that if we believe that it is a great power that has been given, the power to love unconditionally, then we need to find a million ways to effectively communicate it to those whom God sends into lives and have touched us. It is not to be played around with, and I confess it really turns me off when people use the term "I love you" when they mean "I like you." Love is a powerful force, and we will look at it more closely as we go along.

The whole point of the story is to illustrate how important it is to communicate and to check óut to see if our message is being received. I find it hard to understand why we can't ask those whom we really love, "Do you know how much you mean to me?" When we take some-one we love to a meal, or give them a present, pay their college tuition, and so forth, why can't we ask the ques-tion: what does it say to you, about you? You see, the question allows the other the incredible opportunity to internalize your inner message, your gift of love, and that love is at the same moment God's love!

A young friend of mine once told me how he communi-cated his love for his girlfriend in the midst of others. He would merely say to her, "Do you know what?" The an-swer was, I love you! That has become the question that I raise to those who have entered and touched my life, "Do you know what?" I remind them that no matter what happens to them on their journey, they need only close their eyes and they'll hear me whispering, "Hey, do you know what?" If they can respond to the question knowing that I love them as they are, I then make sure that they don't stop there, but go on to the significant question: "What does my love tell you about His love for you?"

The author of *The Cloud* maintains that imperfect hu-mility must always precede perfect humility. He states this clearly in the following passages:

> Although I speak of imperfect humility it is not be-cause I place little value on true self-knowledge. Should all the saints and angels of heaven join with all the members of the Church on earth, both religious and lay, at every degree of Christian holiness and pray for my growth in humility, I am certain that it would not profit me as much nor bring me to the perfection of this virtue as quickly as a little self-knowledge. Indeed, it is altogether impossible to arrive at perfect humility without it.

And therefore, do not shrink from the sweat and toil involved in gaining real self-knowledge, for I am sure that when you have acquired it you will very soon come to an experiential knowledge of God's goodness and love.

. . . I wanted you to appreciate the excellence of perfect humility so that you might keep it before your heart as a spur to your love. This is important for both of us. And finally, I have troubled to explain all this because I believe that just knowing about perfect humility will in itself make you more humble. For I often think that ignorance of humility's two degrees occasions a good deal of pride. It is just possible that a little taste of what I have called imperfect humility might lead you to believe that you were already perfectly humble. But you would be badly deceived and, what is more, have actually fallen into the foul mire of conceit. And so, be diligent in striving for this virtue in all its perfection. When a person experiences it, he will not sin then not long afterward.[10]

Perhaps you have experienced, to varying degrees, both sides of the coin of humility. Like myself, you might have been grounded heavily in imperfect humility, but as the author points out, this opens us up to the possibility of coming to know and taste what he calls perfect humility— the unconditional love of God!

As we look at this we can easily begin to identify individuals, whether they be our parents, relatives, teachers, or whoever, and blame them for not having given us a better formation—for failing to be for us in so many ways. Let me share with you a story which left a deep impression on me and one filled with wisdom. One of my brothers built this beautiful home overlooking the sea, and the family decided to gather together for an open house. There was to be a New England clambake, with lobsters and all that goes with it. I was sitting with my father on the porch, overlooking the sea, and he was caught up on the good feelings of the day. He said, "Isn't it great that this kid is starting out in life with this beautiful home—he's starting off where I finished!" He told me how happy he was to have lived to see all of us grow up, to see his grandchildren, and he reflected on how sad he felt when he thought of Mom, who had died when we were young and never saw how things had worked out. She saw only the hard times and the many difficulties that go hand in hand with raising children. As he was basking in these memories and feeling like he was on cloud nine, one of my brothers appeared, holding a drink in his hand. He came onto the porch and said, "Well, here are the two problems of my life!"

My father was Irish, and he had a keen and razor-sharp mind that could cut you to ribbons at any moment, so I immediately began to think of how I could prevent a bad encounter or a hassle that would spoil the party, the whole family reunion. But before I could say anything, my father turned to my brother and said, "Well, let me tell you something, and if your mother were here she would say the same thing. You see, your grandparents weren't perfect, and then we came along and we were certainly not perfect. We probably made a lot of mistakes with each one of you, but now it's your turn, and I pray to God that you will at least make 'new mistakes.' Don't make the same ones we've made. So don't waste your time blaming me, your mother, brother, teachers, the priests, or whoever— get on with life. It is an exciting adventure and remember, make *new mistakes!*"

My brother turned and left without saying anything. I looked at my father in order to congratulate him, because what he had said was pure wisdom, but before I could say anything, he said to me, "That damn fool will never learn!"

We need to learn and not to make the same mistakes that we might feel were made in our own regard as we started our journey. It is time to let go of the past and to take hold of our own journey. Humility is one of the necessary things for the pilgrimage and we need to look at the other—love of one another.

"THE WINDS OF GOD'S GRACE ARE ALWAYS BLOWING, BUT WE MUST MAKE AN EFFORT TO RAISE OUR SAILS."

REFLECTIONS

1. List the most positive things that have happened to you. What does each say to you about yourself?

2. Identify the significant people in your life. What made them significant for you?

3. What have you learned on your journey in and through relationships? Can you identify some mistakes you made or your parents made? Do you continue to make the same mistakes?

SUGGESTED READINGS

1. William Johnston (ed.). *The Cloud of Unknowing.* Image Books/Doubleday, 1973.

2. John Powell. *Why Am I Afraid to Tell You Who I Am?* Argus Communications, 1969.

CHAPTER III

LOVE OF ONE ANOTHER

In the last chapter we saw that the author of *The Cloud* held that there were only two things that were necessary for the journey: humility and love of one another. Whoever has acquired these two virtues has all that is needed —nothing else is required!

It seems so simple, and yet most of us look for much more. You might have wondered why he put humility first. There is an old Latin saying, *Nemo dat quod non habet,* which means that you can't give what you don't possess. So, unless the two sides of the coin of humility are yours, it is very difficult to go on to love others according to the commandment of Christ. Our feeble attempts to love without first having humility are often, if not always, tied to conditions and we attached strings to our gift, consciously and unconsciously. Often we experience hurt and even rejection as we attempt to reach out and love others, demanding that they fulfill every conceivable need that we have. This is not love. Humility embraces self-knowledge, love of self, and the awareness of the light and darkness that dwells within us. It is from this ground that we can honestly enter relationships that call us to loving and being loved.

C. S. Lewis, in his book *The Four Loves,* sets before us a clear picture of the challenge we face. He says:

> . . . If the Victorians needed the reminder that love is not enough, older theologians were always saying very loudly that (natural) LOVE IS likely to be a great deal too much. The danger of loving our fellow creatures too little was less present to their minds than that of loving them idolatrously. In every wife, mother, child and friend they saw a possible rival to God.
>
> There is one method of dissuading us from inordinate love of the fellow-creature which I find myself forced to reject at the very outset. I do so with trembling, for it met me in the pages of a great saint and a great thinker to whom my own glad debts are incalculable.
>
> In the words, which can still bring tears to the eyes, St. Augustine describes the desolation in which the death of his friend Nebridius plunged him (Confessions IV, 10). Then he draws a moral. This is what comes, he says, of giving one's heart to anything but God. All human beings pass away. Do not let your happiness depend on something you may lose. If love is to be a blessing, not a misery, it must be for the only Beloved who will never pass away.
>
> Of course this is excellent sense. Don't put your goods in a leaky vessel. Don't spend too much on a house you may be turned out of. And there is no man alive who responds more naturally than I to such canny maxims. I am a safety-first creature. Of all the arguments against love, none makes so strong an appeal to

my nature as "Careful! This might lead you to suffering."

To my nature, my temperament, yes. Not to my
conscience. When I respond to that appeal, I seem to
myself to be a thousand miles away from Christ. If I am
sure of anything, I am sure that His teaching was never
meant to confirm my congenial preference for safe
investments and limited liabilities. I doubt whether
there is anything in me that pleases Him less. And who
could conceivably begin to love God on such a pruden-
tial ground—because the security (so to speak) is better? Who could even include it among the grounds for
loving? Would you choose a wife or a friend—if it
comes to that, would you choose a dog—in this spirit?
One must be outside the world of love, of all loves,
before one thus calculates. Eros, lawless Eros, prefer-
ring the Beloved to happiness, is more like Love Himself than this.

I think that this passage in the Confessions is less a
part of St. Augustine's Christendom than a hangover
from the high-minded Pagan philosophies in which he
grew up. It is closer to Stoic "apathy" or neo-Platonic
mysticism than to charity. We follow One who wept
over Jerusalem and at the grave of Lazarus, and, loving
all, yet had one disciple who, in a special sense, he
"loved." St. Paul has a higher authority with us than St.
Augustine. St. Paul, who shows no sign that he would
not have suffered like a man, and no feeling that he
ought not so to have suffered, if Epaphroditus had died
(Philippians 2:27).

Even if it were granted that insurances against
heartbreak were our highest wisdom, does God Him-

self offer them? Apparently not. Christ comes at last to say, "Why hast thou forsaken me?"[1]

Lewis describes for us some of the views that have arisen from the Victorians, older theologians, Augustine, the pagan philosophies, and others that have had their impact on theology and on ourselves. When we read history we sometimes deceive ourselves into thinking that it is the past and that we have not been affected by it. Quite the contrary! Our own history flows out of past history, and either consciously or unconsciously we are often affected by views and concepts of bygone days. One of the great blessings of studying history, especially the development of conceptual frameworks, we can examine them in the light of our own time, accepting them or rejecting them in the light of development. Whatever we choose to do we ultimately must pay the price for our views and how they affect our daily lives. Each of you has a view of love, and it is well worth the effort, toil, and whatever is needed to surface it, examine it, and make sure that it is yours. You must take ownership, and this is made possible through reflection and prayer. Of course, you're free not to do so and allow yourself to live out a viewpoint that might not be grounded in the light of Christ or our rich heritage. The choice is yours!

I will often hear people who are facing the necessity of changing their view state, "Well, I guess everything I did in the past was wrong." The truth of the matter is that as we proceed on our journey, we are accountable only for the "light" we have. The fact that the Holy Spirit is alive in the Church and continually is unfolding a deeper meaning of the Gospel message and enlightening us through the ongoing advance of insights from other sciences makes it imperative that we continually are willing to let go of our views and to change. In looking at the vast amount of knowledge that is available to us today, which has impacted our views and required each of us to change, it is impossible to understand how one could think that one should have known all of this in the past. We can only follow the light we have at each point of our pilgrimage, and if you're open and willing to change when necessary, then you're on the right path and the Holy Spirit will not fail you.

All of us have had to undergo a tremendous amount of change in viewpoints during our lives. Those of us who are older can recall a time of little change and hence great stability, while our young feel that everything is up for grabs, everything changes! As I look back on my own life, there was a period of time where everything seemed to be very secure—a question led to a neat little answer and then to a period—that was it! And God help you if you had another question! It seems that the security of those days led to order, and a clear definition of right and wrong, and for some there is a driving need to return to those times— wipe out everything that has taken place since then and return to the "basics," then we'll have everything once again.

I recall the first time that I was confronted with the option to change. I say option because God never forces us to change or to grow. He leaves us free to respond or not to, and for me it was quite difficult. During my basic training in the Navy we were assembled one day for a lecture by the chaplains. The Catholics went to one hall and the Protestants to another. At one point of the lecture, the chaplain told us that we could eat meat on Friday. My immediate reaction was "I'm in the wrong hall!" After the conference, I approached the chaplain in order to be sure he was a priest. When I asked, he responded, "Yes, I'm

Father O'Malley." He then reassured me that I could eat meat on Friday—wherever I was. As servicemen, we were dispensed from the obligation.

Well, the first time I ate meat on Friday, I had a difficult time. In fact, I believe I went back to the priest to check it out once again. Those of you who are older perhaps can remember the difficulties you faced when changes took place, i.e., the change in the Eucharistic fast from midnight; the change allowing us to drink liquids before communion; the change in the laws and rules of abstinence, fasting, and so forth; changes in the liturgy; and many others. Some of these changes we welcomed with open arms and had little difficulty in accepting. There were others, perhaps, which were a little too sacred to us personally to change, and here we found great difficulty. We are quite adept in picking and choosing the areas we want to change. However, the real task that each of us faces is to remain open to the Holy Spirit, and the need to be willing to *let go* and remain ever faithful to the unfolding richness and understanding of the message of Christ as that Light speaks to us mainly in and through the Church, but also through the knowledge that we are given in other ways. When we do look back we should be able to say that we tried to follow the light that was given to us—that's all that is needed and all that you're capable of doing. The journey is an unfolding mystery, embracing a process of growth into the fullness of the life of Christ, and we must depend on Him for the Light we need to follow Him. He will never fail us!

Perhaps, like myself, you too can identify things that you once held to be infallible, only to find later on you changed your view. It is important to realize that the principles don't change. Hopefully, we grow in our understanding of them, and yet the application of the principles shifts due to many influences that are a result of development. We continually are offered new insights into the message of Christ and our heritage, which allow us to challenge the world with a freshness and speak to it with meaning—not outdated views and expressions of them. It is indeed amazing, startling, when one thinks of the impact of religious viewpoints on our lives and yet how few there are who spend time keeping abreast of this very important area of their lives. We often attend workshops, lectures, and seminars to keep us abreast of our given fields of occupation in order to remain relevant! How much more should we be willing to stay relevant in our understanding of the present-day meaning of the Gospels and in living His way of life in our daily rounds of existing? My brothers are all professional men and very competent in their respective fields. However, it continually amazes me to hear that they will usually say to my nephews and nieces when discussing religious themes, "Wait till your uncle comes home!" Or still better, "I can't explain it, I just believe!" It is not all their fault, certainly the Church has a major responsibility in helping the laity, not to mention priests and religious, to continually grow in their ability to articulate the Good News in the "marketplace." Certainly, it is self-evident that one of the critical challenges of the Church today is formation and adult education.

St. Paul deals with this in another way when he speaks of the need of transformation (Ga 3:27). He identifies that in every transformation there is something left behind and yet there is also a positive gain. In this he implies that there are two aspects that characterize the Christian's journey, a journey that embraces a commitment to a life-long process of conversion. One aspect can be described as negative, in that we let go of views, values, and habits that once gave us meaning. The other aspect is positive, in that our new views, values, and habits that replace the old bring us to a deeper freedom by which we can more fully respond to God as He reveals Himself in our daily lives.

We grow up in an environment that has its own peculiar psychological, sociological, and cultural factors which can open or limit and restrict our views, give or not give direction which makes our response to Christ's call specific and unique. We breathe in various biases and prejudices as we grow up, and each society has its own—they are within each of us. Moreover, they can actually block us and prevent us from seeing life in a broader dimension, in a fuller way, and become obstacles to our Christian journey. We continually find ourselves driven to find the right way, the how-to, and much energy can be spent on this activity. Karl Rahner tells us that there is no recipe for the Christian life being lived out, no possibility of giving a theoretical definition to the law of life of the individual Christian, not to mention the gift granted by the Spirit to the individual, to specific generations, or to the Church. "All that is possible . . . is to perceive vocational imperatives. The response of the Christian embraces some form of asceticism (discipline) which enables him to become free. Free, not in order to wall up his heart but to give it away, to God and to the world."[2]

Whether you call it conversion, transformation, change of viewpoints, it all boils down to the fact that we are called to grow and all growth involves letting go! This letting go requires discernment, and indeed one must be careful not to get caught up in the ever-changing winds, which is not what we are describing. What I am saying is that one must embrace the search for the meaning of His call and, when necessary, be free to let go of whatever might block us from a fuller life in Him.

Love is so key to the Christian life that any misunderstanding of it can have disastrous consequences. Thus the
need to look at your viewpoint and to be sure that it is
grounded on the insights from the Scriptures, our spiritual heritage, and the light we have today.

When I find myself searching for some insights, I often
will pick out an author whom I respect and let the book
just open to a given page and begin to read. On one
occasion that I did this, I found myself reaching out to
Cardinal Newman and picked up his *Book of Sermons.*
The book opened to the page that gave his sermon on the
feast of St. John. In that sermon, he dealt with the injunction that "we should love all men equally." He pointed out
that it was impossible to begin by loving everyone
equally. We must begin to love someone, especially those
close to us, and by loving that one we will then be able to
reach out to another—on and on, which by the end of our
journey perhaps we will have reached the point when we
can love everyone equally. It is, as he points out, in loving
someone that we can send a ripple across the lake—we
can touch many others by taking the risk to love someone.

Again, in *The Four Loves,* Lewis vividly points out that
we can't escape along the lines of Augustine or others who
would stress that we are not to "get too involved in love,"
when he says:

> There is no safe investment. To love at all is to be
> vulnerable. Love anything, and your heart will cer-
> tainly be wrung and possibly be broken. If you want to
> make sure of keeping it intact, you must give your
> heart to no one, not even to an animal. Wrap it care-
> fully round with hobbies and little luxuries; avoid all
> entanglements; lock it up safe in the casket or coffin of
> your selfishness. But in that casket—safe, dark, motion-

less, airless—it will change. It will not be broken; it will become unbreakable, impenetrable, irredeemable. The alternative to tragedy, or least to the risk of tragedy, is damnation. The only place outside Heaven where you can be perfectly safe from all the dangers and perturbations of love is Hell.[3]

I believe that many of us can identify times when we tried to love in a safe way, or, as they used to say, "supernaturally." This attempt to be safe usually arises from the times that we have, as they say, "fumbled the ball"—we've made mistakes and have often been hurt in the process. There are times when we think we are loving, only to discover that we are really operating out of our own needs, out of selfishness. All of this constitutes the ordinary way that we grow in self-knowledge, and it takes both failures and successes to learn and grow in the art of love. The hurt and pain that we often feel comes from various sources, but most often from the knowledge and experience that we either have not loved, or when we have loved that love has not been accepted. Needless to say, relationships of love can at times involve betrayal of secrets and confidences, which bring great pain. At these times one can tragically fall into the trap of building a wall around us to protect us from ever again being hurt, misunderstood, rejected, or making mistakes and when we succumb to this temptation we are, in the words of C. S. Lewis, on the road to hell!

It is safe to say that each of us would like to become a great lover, free to love and be loved, free from our wounded selves, and above all possessing every virtue which would insure that our love was always "pure and beautiful." Some decide to wait until they have it all put together before they'll risk loving. Lewis enlightens us further in this regard by explaining how human love is the very expression of the love of God when he says:

> I believe that the most lawless and inordinate loves are less contrary to God's will than a self-invited and self-protected lovelessness. It is like hiding the talent in a napkin and for much the same reason. "I knew thee that thou wert a hard man." Christ did not teach and suffer that we might become, even in the natural loves, more careful of our own happiness. If a man is not uncalculating towards the earthly beloveds whom he has seen, he is none the more likely to be so towards God whom he has not seen. We shall draw nearer to God, not by trying to avoid sufferings inherent in all loves, but by accepting them and offering them to Him; throwing away all defensive armour. If our hearts need to be broken, and if He chooses this as the way in which they should be broken, so be it.[4]

Love is bound up in friendship. St. Aelred, a Cistercian abbot who wrote the classic on Christian friendship in the twelfth century, saw the Christian life essentially as growth into freedom and the perfection of friendship. When his friend Yvo rendered the text of St. John as "God is friendship," Aelred did not hesitate to add, "He who dwells in friendship dwells in God and God in him."[5] For those who would never respond to the invitation of friendship and enter into "a most sacred kind of love" he held out little hope. "They are no better than the beasts, who give the name of life without friendship, without loving and being loved." St. Bernard and St. Aelred both saw how important friendship was in grounding one's life and in growing into the fullness of the Christian life. To refuse the love of another, to receive coupled with a refusal to give love, will inevitably bring death to the soul.

"Friendship is like a step to raise us to the love and knowledge of God." Aelred goes even further when he stresses that "friendship lies close to perfection." I believe that every pilgrim thirsts to taste and experience these fruits of friendship, but few seem willing to pay the price!

Jesus reveals to us in the Gospel of St. John what friendship is about and gives us a glimpse of the price to be paid. He tells us that He chose us (Jn 15:16), indicating that friendship is first and foremost a choice. He calls us friends (Jn 15:15), and tells us why we are to be friends rather than servants. We are friends because He has revealed everything to us. He has been completely open and shared with us all that is His. What is it to be a friend? He tells us that real friendship involves a radical commitment. "No one can have greater love than to lay down his life for his friends" (Jn 15:13). And finally, He tells us how we can respond to His gift of love, of friendship: "You are my friends, if you do what I command you. . . . My command to you is to love one another" (Jn 15:14, 17).

Jesus tells us what is involved in friendship with Him and with one another. Like Him, we each are free to choose another, extend our gift of love/friendship within an environment of freedom, leaving the other free to accept or reject the gift, the invitation. When the other responds from freedom and the mutual gift of love has been exchanged, then we, following the model given to us by Christ, begin the process of sharing—sharing all! There is a rhythm to this process of sharing, a listening to the invitation, the right moment—there is a mutual flow. It is what in the earlier days they called the exercise of the "art" of love and friendship, which we will look at more closely later on.

True love and friendship, though we each thirst for it, is indeed scary, since it involves a radical *commitment!* The radical, total commitment that Jesus calls us to is the reality that one must be willing to lay down one's life for one's friend. This brings friendship, love of one another, out of the realm of the *temporary:* a friend today, gone tomorrow! No! Friendship involves a total commitment. This is expressed in a poetic way in the currently popular book among the young *The Little Prince.* "When you tame [love] someone, you become responsible forever." Every time I tell another that I love him/her, I have in fact put my life on the line, not just for a moment when I feel good, but forever! I literally am saying to the other, "I am willing to attempt to respond to you with all that I am and have without boundaries or limitations, within the context of my vocational commitments." True, we cannot always be for another what we would like to be, or what they might like, because of other responsibilities that we have assumed—that is, marriage, priesthood, religious life. Nonetheless, true friendship flowers in the environment we provide for one another, an environment of trust and honesty.

Not long ago I read that current research shows that some 87 percent of men report that they have "never experienced intimacy." I found this shocking, and yet it perhaps shows us why there are so many divorces and broken homes in our society today. Women do so much better than men in this area of their lives, and perhaps this reflects the cultural impact on us which puts a great emphasis on boys to be "macho"! Such an emphasis tends to put men out of touch with the feminine side of their personalities, unable to share or express their deepest feelings. I recall that when I was a young boy it was normal to sit in my father's lap, to kiss him, and he was comfortable in throwing me up in his arms and catching me, hugging and kissing me—expressing the love he had for me. However, when I reached adolescence, he announced that men didn't do those things and that we expressed our love with one another through a pat on the back or a firm handshake. But, in fact, it meant that the intimacy that I once had with him was gone.

On my seventeenth birthday, when I was sworn into the Navy, my father walked with me to the South Station in Boston to catch the train for basic training. When it came time to say good-bye, I wanted to embrace him. I could feel the tears surfacing, but before I could do or say anything, he extended his hand and left me after saying, "This was your decision and I expect you to live up to it—God bless you!" When I got on the train, I began to cry and had a difficult time in trying to be a man, trying to hide my pain from the other young men who were with me. I never found out how my father dealt with his feelings, but I feel sure that he too was crying. It took me a long time to discover that I needed to let go of the macho model and get in touch with the feminine side of my own personality. There is no one who is pure masculine or feminine: we are a mix. The challenge for each of us is to become comfortable with ourselves, to take ownership of all our qualities that flow from our masculinity and femininity. I found it to be a difficult challenge and one that I still struggle with. I remember one time a college student came to see me. He began to cry, and without thinking I said, "Pat, don't cry!" He looked up at me and said, "Vince, what's wrong with crying?" Inside I laughed at myself, and told him he could cry all he wanted to, and it was beautiful that he could express himself.

Intimacy is essential for each of us, and it is not "going to bed with someone"—in fact, there are too many people

today who associate intimacy with sexuality and sadly discover that it doesn't bring them to intimacy. It can be an
expression of intimacy, but is not necessary for intimacy.
St. Aelred tells us that you can have love without friendship, but you can't have friendship without love, since
friendship embraces much more than love—it embraces
intimacy. Intimacy, for St. Aelred and the other mystics, is
that deep sharing that takes place between friends. As St.
Ambrose says, "A friend hides nothing." No doubt, at this
very moment, you can identify individuals whom you love
but whom you would not share everything with, for whatever reasons, and yet with a friend you'd be comfortable
in sharing whatever you wanted to share and know that it
would be treasured by the friend.

In our present society one of the major challenges that
the Church faces is, in my estimation, once again becoming a School of Love and Friendship. Pope Paul VI inti-
mated this in his first encyclical when he described the
need for the art of spiritual communication. Love of one
another, friendship, is an art! Like any other art, it is
developed and perfected in relation of master to disciple,
in disciplined practice, in making mistakes, in being open
to honesty, and in the challenge to grow.

In exploring the commandment "Love one another," I
believe much is to be gained by looking at it within the
framework of friendship. Aelred maintains that "scarcely
any happiness whatever can exist among mankind without friendship, and man is to be compared to a beast if he
has no one to rejoice with him in adversity, no one to
whom to unburden his mind if any annoyance crosses his
path or with whom to share some unusually sublime or
illuminating inspiration. 'Woe to him that is alone, for
when he falls, he has none to lift him up.' (Eccles. 4:10) He
is entirely alone who is without a friend."[6] He, like other

men and women in our heritage, extols the incredible gift of friendship, and you can readily see that each of us yearns to find this precious gift. Aelred says, "What happiness, what security, what joy to have someone to whom you dare speak on terms of equality as to another self; one to whom you can unblushingly make known what progress you have made in the spiritual life; one to whom you can entrust all the secrets of your heart and before whom you can place all your plans! What, therefore, is more pleasant than so to unite to oneself the spirit of another and of two to form one, that no boasting is thereafter to be feared, no suspicion to be dreaded, no correction of one by the other to cause pain, no praise on the part of one to bring a charge of adulation from the other."[7] "A loyal friend," says the Wise Man, "is the elixir of life" (Si 6:16).

St. Thomas Aquinas stated that all knowledge and love of God is based on analogy—on the human. For Aelred, Bernard, Ambrose, Anselm, Teresa of Ávila, and so many other mystics, saints, and spiritual authors the ultimate test for each of us is: How do we relate to one another? As Aelred says, "Friendship is a stage bordering upon that perfection which consists in the love and knowledge of God, so that man from being a friend of his fellowman becomes the friend of God. According to the words of the Savior in the Gospel, 'I will not now call you servants, but my friends.' (Jn 15:15)"[8]

Which one of us, at some point or another, hasn't experienced that what we perceived to be friendship came to an end. When this happens there is a great deal of pain, wondering how we failed or what we could have done to preserve the relationship. However, as Aelred points out, friendship is much more, and true friendship can never end.

. . . a friend is called a guardian of love or, as some
would have it, a guardian of the spirit itself. Since it is
fitting that my friend be a guardian of our mutual love
or the guardian of my own spirit so as to preserve all its
secrets in faithful silence, let him, as far as he can cure
and endure such defects as he may observe it: let him
rejoice with his friend in his joys, and weep with him in
his sorrows, and feel as his own all that his friend experiences . . .[9]

Friendship, therefore, is that virtue by which spirits are
bound by ties of love and sweetness, and out of many are
made one. Even the philosophers of this world have
ranked friendship not with things casual or transitory but
with the virtues which are eternal. Solomon in the Book of
Proverbs appears to agree with them when he says, "He
that is a friend loves at all times," manifestly declaring
that friendship is eternal if it is true friendship, but, if it
should ever cease to be, then it was not true friendship,
even though it seemed to be so.

. . . remember this: he was never a friend who
could offend him whom he at one time received into
his friendship; on the other hand, that other has not
tasted the delights of true friendship who even when
offended has ceased to love him whom he once cherished. For "he that is a friend loves at all times." Although he be accused unjustly, though he be injured,
though he be cast in the flames, though he be crucified,
"he that is a friend loves at all times." Our Jerome
speaks similarly: "A friendship which can cease was
never true friendship."[10]

We use the term friendship loosely, to say the least, and I believe that some of the difficulties that arise are due to the fact that we just don't grasp the fullness, the responsibilities, and the depth of what it means to be a friend. From the fifth to the twelfth century, the Irish tradition referred to true friendship as "a soul-friend." There was a saying in those days that a person without a soul-friend was like a body without a head—no place to go on the journey!

Today most people would distinguish between different kinds of friendships, and Aelred says that they fall into three categories. The first two, carnal and worldly, are at times mistaken for true friendship, which he identifies only with spiritual friendship.

Individuals who enter this gate of carnal relationships seeking the answer to their hunger for inner meaning and true friendship will find only tragedy—broken human beings driven, as they say, from one high to another. They are driven by lust and the desire to satisfy their needs for affection and sex. People become "objects," like an ice cream cone, to be enjoyed and thrown away. There is no honesty, no commitment, and certainly no responsibility to one another. Most of us on our journey have experienced this kind of relationship and know that it is empty and meaningless. Yet, such an experience can offer us the ability to emerge much stronger and get on with what life is meant to be. The old abbot used to say that there are two ways of learning: one is to sit at the feet of a master; the other way is through experience. The ideal is to embrace both, but I confess in my own life I have learned mostly in and through experience, especially my mistakes.

As we search for this hidden treasure, true friendship, we sometimes enter different gates seeking the treasure.

Another possible gate that we might enter is what he calls worldly relationships. Here we have the fair-weather type, those who choose to foster a relationship with you in order to use you. You become an object which they use to profit financially, socially, or in any way that will improve their status or assist them in their goals. This kind of relationship is more difficult to perceive than carnal relationships, and you usually know only when the person has gained what they want from having used you and walked out of your life. Of course, such experiences leave scars and can make you very dubious and suspicious. Here you must be careful not to put up a steel wall to protect yourself, lest in so doing you shut out the very one who can be a true friend.

We usually experience both of the above types of relationships, and they can help us to continue our search for the real thing—spiritual friendship, soul-friendship. The gate is indeed narrow and few seem to find their way to it, but when one does pass through this gate one enters into the pasture where one finds meaning, fulfillment, and that deep inner peace which comes from following the Master. It is the flowering of our efforts to continue trying to "love one another"! Aelred places before us the depth, richness, and beauty found in soul friendship, true friendship, when he says:

> And praying to Christ for his friend, and longing to be heard by Christ for his friend's sake, he reaches out with devotion and desire to Christ himself. And suddenly and insensibly, affection passing into affection, as though touched by the gentleness of Christ close at hand, he begins to taste how sweet he is and to feel how lovely he is. Thus, from the holy love with which he embraces his friend, he rises to that by which he

embraces Christ. It is as it were only a step to heaven
where God is all in all.[11]

Our rich heritage in this area of friendship is capti-
vating, exciting, and challenging. I recall as a young monk
when I was first introduced to the writings of Aelred by
the prior of my monastery, Father Edward McCorkle,
who later became the abbot of our monastery in Virginia,
how difficult it was to end our discussions. I was too ex-
cited and couldn't wait for our next meeting.

The years have passed and I still find myself returning
to the sources and pondering them again and again, each
time finding myself to be challenged and also full of hope
and motivation. However, to make it all one's own is the
work of a lifetime, and no matter how many times you feel
the urge to quit, you must keep getting up and infallibly
one day you discover the pearl of great value, true friendship. When you arrive at that moment of your journey,
then you'll know that in soul friendship you have found
everything. The hurts, mistakes, betrayals, and everything else that has befallen you on the journey seems like
nothing. I myself have found that it is indeed worth a
million betrayals of all sorts, and as a result of not quitting,
to have found a true friend.

When Aelred says that you can have love without
friendship, but never friendship without love, I believe
that this insight has something to say to us today about the
necessary preparation for marriage. I remember one evening a young man met me for dinner to talk about his
divorce. As he shared with me I became aware that there
was no real friendship between husband and wife. However, he did love her, and this caused considerable difficulty for the wife, who couldn't quite put that together
with their divorce. When I shared with him Aelred's com-

ment on love and friendship and pointed out that friendship always embraced intimacy, whereas you can love
someone and not have intimacy, his eyes lit up and he
said, "That's it! We were never friends!" It seems to me
that marriage is above all a call to the life of soul friendship, and we need to help young people to see this. Those
who are married need a great deal of ongoing help in
supporting their relationship and helping them to develop and perfect the "art" of friendship and spiritual
communication.

Today we hear such phrases as "falling in love" and "I
love you," but in many cases such phrases are describing
strong feelings of affection for the other person, even
love, but not friendship. Aelred says:

> . . . we embrace very many with every affection,
> but yet in such a way that we do not admit them to the
> secrets of friendship, which consist especially in the
> revelation of all our confidences and plans. Whence it
> is that the Lord in the Gospel says: "I will not now call
> you servants but friends", and then adding the reason
> for which they are considered worthy of the name of
> friend: "because all things whatsoever I have heard of
> my Father, I have made known to you." From these
> words, as St. Ambrose says, "He gives the formula of
> friendship for us to follow: namely, that we do the will
> of our friend, that we disclose to our friend whatever
> confidences we have in our hearts, and that we be not
> ignorant of his confidences. Let us bare to him our
> heart and let him disclose his to us. For a friend hides
> nothing. If he is true, he pours forth his soul just as the
> Lord Jesus pored forth the mysteries of the Father."
> Thus speaks Ambrose. How many, therefore, do we
> love before whom it would be imprudent to lay bare

our souls and pour out our inner hearts! Men whose
age, or feeling, or discretion is not sufficient to bear
such revelations.[12]

I think that in the language of today true friendship is the
ability to "stand naked" before one's friend—there are no
secrets; both the dark and the light sides of our personality
are known by our friend. Of course, you can see how scary
that can be, and I think this is because of the incredible
"power" we give to the other—the power to accept and
affirm us and at the same time the power to reject and
seemingly destroy us. Therefore, the temptation is to enjoy the lighter side—that is, to discuss common interests;
to teach or learn from one another; to have a good time at
the bar, sharing stories; to love being with another, receiving their love, but all the time avoiding anything that
would touch the real depths of our being. Yes, we miss the
person, we enjoy their presence, and the times we spend
together are rewarding, but Aelred says that such "friendship except for the trifles and deception, if nothing dis-
honorable enters into it, is to be tolerated in the hope of
more abundant grace, as the beginnings, so to say, of a
holier friendship. By these beginnings, with a growth in
piety and in constant zeal for things of the spirit, with the
growing seriousness of maturer years and the illumination
of the spiritual senses, they may, with purer affections,
mount to loftier heights from, as it were, a region close by,
just as we said the friendship of man could be easily translated into a friendship for God himself because of the
similarity existing between both."[13]
Love is indeed a powerful force, and it always leads to
some form of the expression of our affections. In dealing
with our affections, we must endeavor to ensure that they
flow with respect for the other, and we must find in the

relationship that vehicle which is both proper and fitting to communicate our love. One must always be sensitive to the right moment, in touch with oneself, listening to the invitation of the other, and striving to be honest, if one hopes to have the communication of affection an affirming experience. When one finally embraces a true friend, a soul-friend, then and then alone does one experience and taste the depths and fullness of the Christian way of life. "True friendship is a foretaste of heaven, where no one hides his thoughts or disguises his affection. This is that true and everlasting friendship, which begins here and is perfected there. Here, few know it, where few are good. There, everyone shares it, where all are good. Even in this world, where not all we love can be our friends, how much easier it is to live in an atmosphere of love and trust, rather than surrounded by every kind of suspicion, loving no one and feeling oneself to beloved by no one."[14]

Humility and *love of one another* are the two things that we need to make the journey to the Father. The journey begins at birth and continues through death to the resurrection, and during that pilgrimage each of us, in some way, relives the life of Christ. We are given the freedom to respond to His invitation at each and every moment of the journey as the paschal mystery unfolds in our own lives. And, as the author of *The Cloud* says, "The only other one He needs, is You." To continually say *"Yes!"* You will fall, make mistakes, and yes, even sin, but as the spiritual authors say, if you *never quit—never give up,* you can rest assured that God will infallibly bring you to the mountain and then you'll see that what St. Paul said is true: "All things work out for those who love!" As I so often say, too good to be true, but true!

The journey can be short or long, and no doubt there will be times of discouragement and you'll feel deep down, what's the use? The old abbot used to say to me that one important task is to tie a knot at the end of the rope, and when you reach the knot hang on and never let go! Don't give way to discouragement, and put your trust and hope in the Lord, who will never fail you. Each day brings new opportunities and by continually trying we will finally win. My spiritual director, before I entered the monastery, was indeed a master, and I later discovered that the old abbot considered him to be one of the finest spiritual directors on the east coast. Monsignor Dwyer, no relation, opened me to the richness of our spiritual heritage, guided me, and gave me so much. He is now a retired priest, but will always be a part of me. Over these years I have tried to share with others what he taught me. He once said to me that there was only *one* question you should ask on your journey, "Am I trying?" Never ask yourself the question "Did I succeed?" and certainly not the question "Could I have tried harder?"

The question concerning success is deeply rooted in our society, but it has nothing to do with the spiritual life, since success depends upon situations, circumstances, other people, and God Himself—none of whom you have any control over—so it's a dumb question. The question that deals with the past is also a dumb question to ask, since you're taking the light you now have and applying it to the past when you didn't have it. It took me a long time to digest this simple rule, and I can only share with you from my experience that if you ask either or both of the dumb questions then the trapdoor will open and the manure will come down on your head! Hold on to the one valid question, Am I trying? In being able to respond to that question with a yes, you'll one day find yourself on the mountain, viewing everything from a different perspective and the words of Augustine will ring true, "All things work out for those who TRY to love!"

"THE WINDS OF GOD'S GRACE ARE ALWAYS BLOWING, BUT WE MUST MAKE AN EFFORT TO RAISE OUR SAILS."

REFLECTIONS

1. What qualities in a friendship have been the most important for you?

2. Do you have a soul-friend? What does that relationship mean to you?

3. Identify some relationships in which you gave yourself only to be betrayed, or have the relationship just end. What did you learn from these relationships?

SUGGESTED READINGS

1. C. S. Lewis. *The Four Loves.* Harcourt, Brace, 1960.

2. Aelred of Rievaulx. *On Spiritual Friendship.* Cistercian Publications, 1977.

3. Louis Monden. *Sin, Liberty, and Law.* Sheed & Ward, 1965.

4. Kenneth Leech. *Soul-Friend.* Harper & Row, 1977.

CHAPTER IV

THE LIFE OF DIALOGUE

Humility and Love of One Another is the ground, the very foundation from which we are called to live out the Gospel. The Church, down through the centuries, has given directives which are rooted in Her basic desire to see each of us embrace the total message of Christ and to judge all things according to the Gospel. Each generation, however, faces the task of making the message of Christ relevant, for as Rahner says, "Truly realized Christianity is always the achieved synthesis on each occasion of the message of the gospel and of the grace of Christ, on the one hand, and of the concrete situation in which the gospel is to be lived, on the other."[1]

As we look at ourselves, and reflect on the areas we have treated, you can hardly escape the undeniable fact that development, process, is rooted in a principle. We are free to assent or not, but we can't avoid the fact of development, change, evolution, growth. Today, as perhaps never before, we live in the midst of changing situations and must come to accept this fact. In our relationships with one another, with the world we live in, and with God, we must always be open—open to new ways, to new insights, to new life!

Salvation history clearly indicates that we are always left free to make choices, to orient our lives in one direction rather than in another. This option is critical for the Christian, for as Louis Monden in his book *Sin, Liberty, and Law* states, "the choice among many objects offers an infinite number of possibilities; the fundamental option is made between a 'yes' and a 'no' in which man, as a spirit, unconditionally commits or refuses himself. That option always amounts to letting oneself go: either yielding to a 'becoming,' to a growing towards a more perfect self-realization and new risk."[2] It thus can be seen that this basic choice that we are talking about is of the essence of our fulfillment, without which we can only flounder and drift. As Monden says, we must meet this fundamental responsibility "in order to realize itself this basic option must enter into a dialogue with a complete psycho-physical situation and development, assume all required determinisms within its free directedness and thus bestow on them, out of the freedom, a new shape for the future."[3]

It is this type of option that is the ground from which the Christian grows and develops. Revelation tells us of the relation of intimacy to which God calls us, but in order to enter that intimacy one must make the crucial, fundamental option. Often this basic commitment is called conversion. It places each of us in a dynamic relationship, we are initiated into a state and process of grace and communion with God by this radical decision. All through the New Testament we are being asked to choose, to make a decision and to enter a relational process of change and development.

A free human choice is made only when it springs from a much deeper root than ordinary actions, when the choice is with respect to our whole being, setting the direction and the meaning of your life. From this point of view you can see that no responsible person can treat lightly or avoid facing the need to determine the direction of his/her journey, without serious consequences. As I mentioned earlier, it seems to me, that one of the major problems in our society is that individuals avoid making such fundamental choices because of the commitment involved and the realization that there is a price to be paid for such choices. The sad thing is that the price to be paid flows not only from commitment, but also from noncommitment.

For those of us who have chosen to follow Christ the possibilities, the options narrow down to a single choice. Yes, you can look at it in many ways, but ultimately you'll have to face the choice between a life of love or a life of selfishness. Another way of looking at it would be the choice of pursuing the path to soul-friendship, or carnal and worldly relationships—between meaning and nonmeaning.

In the Scriptures we encounter God, we enter a relationship with God who personally addresses us, and we personally reply to Him in faith. Faith is our response to the living God disclosing Himself from moment to moment in everyday life. Life then is a relationship in dialogue with the god who lives in each of us and calls us to community.

The term dialogue has become a rather common word these days, and words sometimes lose their clear-stamped image. In the past dialogue had one principle meaning: the exchange of conversation among characters in a novel, play, or narrative poem. As such, the dialogue was artificial in that it was controlled by the artist. In our present time and within the context of what we're about, the term dialogue represents an act of semantic redemption. It has a deep religious connotation.

The real meaning of dialogue is that it attempts to unite, to unite persons who want to be united. Dialogue is realized in an authentic, loving encounter between persons wanting to be one. Pope Paul VI in his encyclical *Paths of the Church*, chooses the term "dialogue" as a vehicle to challenge the Christian in the modern world and once again to highlight the relevance of the Good News. He says, "The duty consonant with the patrimony received from Christ is that of spreading, offering, announcing it to others. Well do we know that "Go, therefore, make disciples of all nations," is the last command of Christ to His Apostles (Mt 28:19). By the very term 'Apostles' these men define their inescapable mission. To this internal drive of charity which tends to become the external gift of charity we will give the name of dialogue, which has in these days come into common usage."[4]

Pope Paul VI, in my estimation, attempted many times to focus the attention of the Church, "The People of God," on the need for a deep inner conversion to the Good News, and the need to embrace the rich heritage of the Church which could impact the modern world in its search for the meaning of life. "And did not John XXIII, our immediate predecessor of venerable memory, place an even sharper emphasis on its [The Church's] teaching in the sense of approaching as close as possible to the experience and the understanding of the modern world? And was not the Council itself assigned—and justly so—a pastoral function which would be completely focused on the injection of the Christian message into the stream of the thought, of the speech, of the culture, of the customs, of the strivings of man as he lives today and acts in this life."[5]

"For God sent his Son into the world not to judge the world, but so that through him the world might be saved" (Jn 3:17), and Paul VI states:

> See then, Venerable Brethren, the transcendent origin of the dialogue. It is found in the very plan of God. Religion, of its very nature, is a relationship between God and man. Prayer expresses such a relationship in dialogue. Revelation, i.e., the supernatural relationship which God Himself, on His own initiative, has established with the human race, can be expressed in the Incarnation and therefore in the Gospel.[6]

Our rich heritage, which over and over again tells us of the journey and the need to grow, to change, is found in the proclamation that "the history of salvation narrated exactly this long and changing dialogue which begins with God and brings to man a many-splendored conversation. It is in this conversation of Christ among men that God allows us to understand something of Himself, the mystery of His life, unique in its essence, Trinitarian in its persons; and He tells us finally how He wishes to be known; He is Love; and how He wishes to be honored and served by us: love is our supreme commandment."[7] Here again we find ourselves faced with the free choice to follow Christ in living a life of love, of friendship. "The dialogue thus takes on full meaning and offers ground for confidence. The child is invited to it; the mystic finds a full outlet in it."[8]

Pope Paul VI sets before us not only a challenge but, more important, a way to bring unity and meaning into our lives. It is in and through a life of dialogue. This begins for each of us at birth and ends only when we are united to God in eternal life. Thus dialogue is the vehicle which allows us to discover true friendship with others and with God.

Vatican II surfaced a richness that had been lost—namely, that the Church is not an abstract structure or building, but it is the People of God. In earlier times the Church was identified as people and it was also described as a School of Love and a School of Friendship. Paul VI later on describes dialogue as the art of spiritual communication. This art is very important because it is a skill that we need in order to communicate and to receive the unconditional love of God, who has given each of us this power so that we can grow into the fullness of His life within us.

The training of a dialogical person begins in the family and is the work of a lifetime. When you reflect on your early development you often discover that dialogue and the art of spiritual communication were not always in the forefront. This can be attributed to many causes and yet the absence of the dialogical process has disastrous effects on us. In my own case, I recall that as a young child I began to think I was an orphan. One day I decided to run away from home so I packed a few things and began my exodus. My mother saw me all dressed with my bag coming down the staircase and she began to ascend the staircase. When she reached me, she asked me, "Where are you going?" I replied, "I'm running away from home." With that she sat down on the staircase and invited me to sit next to her. She then said, "Why are you running away?" I told her that I was an orphan. She asked me how I reached that conclusion and I said, "All my brothers have blond hair and blue eyes and I don't belong to you and Dad." She then asked me what color hair she had and I responded, "Brown." "What color eyes do I have?" she asked. I said, "Brown." She then said to me, "You see, you look like me—you have brown hair and brown eyes, and your brothers all look like your father." She went on to share with me that she nearly died giving birth to me. However, when she finished sharing, I said to her, "I don't believe you." With that I went on my journey, but since it was snowing and cold I returned home shortly afterward to a warm hug.

No doubt you can recall times when someone who was significant to you tried to enter dialogue with you, but perhaps like myself you didn't respond or you were not able to open yourself to the richness and depth of love and meaning the other was offering you. However, the challenge to enter this school and to develop the art of spiritual communication remains, and there are indeed many lessons to be learned from reflecting and praying over what it's all about.

Each of us struggles to establish true dialogue and within each family, the primary school of love and friendship, there are successes and failures. As we look at the principles, I ask you to reflect on your own journey and see if you can identify when the principles were operative and also what kind of fruit came forth from such encounters. I emphasize the positive because I believe that we too readily look only at the failures. If you choose to look at the failures, then I ask you to respond to the question: What did you learn?

Paul VI states that "we need to keep ever present this ineffable, yet real relationship of the dialogue which God the Father, through Christ in the Holy Spirit, has offered to us and established with us, if we are to understand the relationship which we, i.e., the Church, should strive to establish and to foster with the human race."[9] In other words, as God reveals Himself and enters dialogue with each of us, so too we must strive to enter and continue this dialogue with one another.

Christ, our model, tells stories and without a doubt one of the greatest challenges we face is to get in touch with our own story and be able to share it. God has chosen to continue the Paschal mystery in the lives of each of us. God continues His real Presence in and through each of us and He asks us to reveal to one another our stories which enhance all the facets of our lives. I'm unique and will never be duplicated, and this also is true of you. The beauty of God, His love, His mercy, His steadfastness in my journey must be revealed in order to encourage others to see and to understand the power of God in their own lives. I'm constantly reminded of the power we have to touch others and to encourage them through sharing our story. People approach me often and tell me how much it meant to them when I revealed my story and more often than not they feel they know me when in fact they met me on a video or TV screen. Storytelling is a powerful vehicle of communicating and it offers the possibility of encountering others in a very meaningful way. It also invites others to share their own story, which always reveals the work of God in our lives. Risky, oh yes, but insofar as we are willing to take the risk and respond to the invitation of self-revelation we are given the power, in and through that process, of revealing the beauty of God within us. We can choose not to enter this risky process of self-revelation and thus refuse to manifest to others the beauty and power of God that has been entrusted to us from all eternity. That would be sad!

Paul VI sets before us six basic points concerning this life of dialogue which he gleaned from meditating on the Scriptures.[10] With each of the six fundamental principles that he sets before us as illustrating how God enters dialogue with us, He challenges Christians likewise to enter dialogue with one another and with the world we live in.

The first principle deals with spontaneity. "The dialogue of salvation was opened spontaneously on the initiative of God: "He (God) loved us first" (I Jn. 4:10), it will be up to us to take the initiative in extending to men this same dialogue, without waiting to be summoned to it."

Spontaneity is very important to the life of dialogue and I discovered that for the greater part of my life I had lost the ability to be spontaneous. When I looked at this, I discovered that this loss was mainly due to the culture that I grew up in which blessed spontaneity in children, but cautioned us as adults. Cautioned us because we can make mistakes. Today, interestingly, research shows that if we could be in touch with our inner spirit and operate from those spontaneous movements, it would be more conducive to our growth and the growth of others than not. One needs only to reflect on this to realize that it is true. Does it really touch you when you receive a postcard from someone who has taken a trip and you know that you are on their list, their program, and that the address label and perhaps even a line or two was already finished, waiting only for the stamp and postmark from their destination? Or does it touch you when, out of nowhere, you receive a card or a phone call from someone who just happened to think of you? I'm sure that you'd agree that it is those spontaneous movements of the Spirit that enable us to touch one another, not programmed activities! Yet it does become a task to rediscover this childlike quality. In fact, I believe you can learn much about the spiritual life and dialogical qualities by observing children. Christ tells us that unless we become like children we cannot enter the kingdom. Spontaneity is essential to the life of true dialogue, and although at times we might make mistakes, we need nevertheless to get in touch with our inner spirit and to try operating from those spontaneous movements.

The second principle of dialogue is that it must be grounded in charity. The dialogue of salvation began with charity, with the divine goodness: "God so loved the world as to give His only-begotten Son" (Jn. 3:16); nothing but fervent and unselfish love should motivate our dialogue."

The third principle deals with an interior attitude that is somewhat foreign to our culture which is so "result"-oriented. "The dialogue of salvation was not proportioned to the merits of those to whom it was directed, nor to the results which it would achieve or fail to achieve: "Those who are healthy need no physician" (Lk. 5:31); so also our own dialogue ought to be without limits or ulterior motives."

So often we enter relationships in order to get results or to fulfill our own needs. When we give way to these tendencies we remove ourselves from dialogue, and once again the effects have serious consequences. I recall that my father articulated a very sound principle when we were growing up. He used to say, "You're all individuals, different, and it is foolish to compare you to one another. However, I ask you to do the best you can and your effort is what is important." That is certainly sound advice and I took him to mean what he said. When it came time to present my report card from school I stressed that I had tried. However, when he looked at the card he responded, "You didn't try and you're grounded!" I discovered that success was important and results were essential. As I grew up this lesson was reinforced in many different ways, and today one can't help but wonder how young people ever discover that true friendship and dialogue are not found through selfish behavior or when we demand results and success.

I suppose that most of us can now look back and see the wisdom of our parents and appreciate them more and more as we get older. It is indeed a very delicate balance between the perception of a parent and that of a child. If we begin to think that we must succeed, and that producing results is essential, then we will suffer a great deal. Life is not just about success and results, important as they may be; there is much more. Christ's proclamation of the unconditional love of the Father is a message that must sink deep within our hearts. From this inner experience, which come to us mainly in and through others, we have a freedom to be. What a challenge to enter a relationship with love and without any demands on the other! It requires tremendous discipline.

The fourth principle articulates the necessity of leaving people free to respond to or reject an invitation.

> The dialogue of salvation did not physically force anyone to accept it; it was a tremendous appeal of love which, although placing a vast responsibility on those toward whom it was directed (cf. Mt. 11:12), nevertheless left them free to respond to it . . . So too, [ours] will not be introduced in the armor of external force, but simply through the legitimate means of human education, of interior persuasion, or ordinary conversation, and it will offer its gift of salvation with full respect for personal and civic freedom.

When you reflect on this you might discover, as I did, that in many relationships we do not leave people free. Every time I enter a relationship I deeply desire a response, and unless I'm careful I attach a string, a rope, to my gift. I then pull the rope in order to get a response, hopefully the one I want. It is one thing to want a response, but it is quite another to demand one. I believe it was St. John of the Cross who said that if you tie a single string to the leg of a bird, the bird will not be able to fly. It is our task to let people "fly" by setting them free! I discovered on my own journey that I had to carry a pair of "mystical scissors," and when I discover my own strings, attachments, wanting to possess another, wanting them to be for me in ways that would leave them bound to me by perceived obligations, then I have to pull out my scissors and cut them free. It is only in the environment of freedom that we grow into the fullness of our unique beauty and gifts.

We are called to create an environment of invitation. In the language of youth, we are to send out "vibes" so that others can receive an invitation to enter a relationship, but always leaving them free to respond or to reject it. It takes great interior discipline to leave people we love very much—FREE!

The fifth principle reminds us that our love cannot be exclusive but must be open to all. "The dialogue of salvation was made accessible to all; it was destined for all without distinction (cf. Col. 3:11); in like manner our own dialogue should be potentially universal . . ."

I find it difficult at times to be open to those who are close to me, let alone to complete strangers. When I reflect on our present situation where people pass each other like ships in the dead of night, neither acknowledging one another nor aware of their presence, I can't help but believe that a growing awareness of the need to be open is an essential ingredient in changing our society. It must begin with those close to us; only then can we extend our circle, finally opening ourselves to the whole world. I travel a great deal and I can attest to the fact that I more often than not want to close my eyes or bury myself in a book rather than be open to the person sitting next to me in the plane. Wearing a Roman collar is like flashing a neon sign inviting people to speak to you, and more than once I've wished that I were in secular dress. However, I confess that it is always an incredible and unforgettable experience when someone feels free to reach out and I'm open to that person. I feel that God put me in that seat just to be for that other person. So we need not be like passing ships, we can try to be brothers and sisters who care about each other, even when they are strangers!

The sixth principle once again challenges our present success-oriented values.

The dialogue of salvation normally experienced a gradual development, successive advances, humble beginnings before complete success (cf. Mt. 13:31). Ours too will take cognizance of the slowness of psychological and historical maturation and of the need to wait for the hour when God may make our dialogue effective. Not for this reason will our dialogue postpone till tomorrow what it can accomplish today; it ought to be eager for the opportune moment; it ought to sense the preciousness of time (cf. Eph. 4:16). Today, i.e., every day, our dialogue should begin again; we, rather than those toward whom it is directed, should take the initiative.

The emphasis and pressure to succeed can have a major impact on our self-concept and self-image. Paul VI stresses that the life of dialogue, true friendship and love, is not based solely on success. If success comes, fine, but that isn't everything. Scripture tells us that even God did not "pull it off" the first time around. God did not succeed and as Paul VI says, "There was a gradual development, successive advances, humble beginnings before complete success."[11] As I pointed out earlier, in the spiritual life there is a different set of questions that have little to do with our cultural values. It is therefore difficult to shift gears and leave behind what the world puts forth as a treasured value, and embrace the "Good News." The only question you should be posing to yourself is, am I trying? Success, as Paul VI points out, depends upon many factors that you have no control over—it is really the work of the Holy Spirit and He will infallibly bring success about, but according to His time and way, not yours or mine.

We must wait for the right timing, always listening to the heart and invitation of the other, which requires great discipline. The life of dialogue is a way of life, and as we grow in this school of love and friendship our horizons open up and we enter a new world, a world in which we are sensitive to all that it embraces. Our only option is to embrace the totality of a life of love. Dialogue is a way of living this life of love, and Paul VI states that "it is an example of the art of spiritual communication."[12]

The deeper meaning of dialogue that we have been looking at is an outgrowth of modern philosophy, especially existential phenomenology. Modern philosophers describe the human person more in line with the existential, dynamic, and personalistic approach. The human person is seen as radically himself/herself in and through personal relationships, "to be" means to be open to the other so that the person becomes himself/herself in relation to the other. It is persons who give meaning to reality. Thinkers like Buber, Marcel, Jaspers, Tournier, Kant, Luijpen, Plattel, Teilhard de Chardin, and Camus see relations between person and person as central to human existence. Process philosophy has also reached the same conclusion: "The 'I' becomes truly a personality when it is united with its 'Thou,' and the greater that union, the greater the personality. Outside the interpersonal union, we have an individual but not a person. Existence, self-hood, or individuality, and meaning are all therefore to be found in the context of union or process."[13]

In the field of psychology and the social sciences, we find an emphasis today and a belief that self-concept and a developing self is related to our interaction with others and the whole environment. "The self is a product of social experience, the result of the behavior of others towards the individual . . . The self develops out of social interaction, and the individual's self-concept is his own definition of his relationship to the world about him."[14] Experience tells each of us that it is in relationships that we encounter life's great satisfactions, as well as our crucial conflicts.

It can thus be seen that dialogue is bound up in "interpersonal relationships," it is that type of interpersonal relationship which is "the response of one's whole being to the otherness of the other, that otherness that is comprehended only when I open myself to him in the present and in the concrete situation and respond to his need even when he himself is not aware that he is addressing me."[15] For Martin Buber, the Jewish philosopher, dialogue is an I-Thou relationship, a relationship of openness and mutuality between persons. If a relationship, a friendship, is characterized by mutuality, directness, intensity, and presence and is valued in itself and not as a means to an end, it is I-Thou. If, on the other hand, it is characterized by possessiveness, exploitation, and indirectness and is valued as a means to an end, the relationship is I-It. From what we have said earlier you can see that what

Aelred called "carnal and worldly" relationships would fall into the I-It world of Buber. Spiritual, soul-friendship, would be the world of I-Thou.

It is important to recognize that genuine dialogue is found in presence, mutual honesty, and openness—it is an encounter and can be found in conversation, silence, in a smile, a wink, and in a thousand other different ways. In this dialogue, just as in our rich heritage of soul-friendship, we find ourselves accepted, affirmed, healed, purified, forgiven and loved, which reunites us with ourselves, with another, and with God. It is here in dialogue, in spiritual friendship, that one truly finds one's self, one's self-worth, and can risk being fully known. We no longer need the masks to wear in order to be accepted or loved for whom we are. This fundamental need is so basic that it becomes the most pressing and crucial, if not the major task of our journey. It is said that all behavior, in varying degrees, can be understood in reference to this basic human need.

In attempting to live a life of dialogue one will discover meaning, and infallibly you'll receive that incredible gift, the gift of a soul-friend. God did not create us to go through life without a soul-friend, and when one walks on the journey alone it is, in my estimation, ultimately because we made a choice not to open ourselves to the risks and the vulnerability of loving another. As I look back on my journey there have been relationships that inflicted great pain, anxieties, confusion, pain, anger, and even bitterness, which often tempted me to never get involved again—never open myself to love or friendship. Now I can say from experience that all the hurts, the betrayals of trust and confidences and the trials that are part and parcel of our journeys are all washed away and disappear into the past when you finally receive the gift of a soul-friend! The only thing that will ever prevent you from receiving the gift is when you give way to the feeling that it just isn't worth it—it's too difficult to be vulnerable, to be open, to be loving and you turn to walk down the path of anger, bitterness, and finally cynicism. You've lost your way and there is no meaning in your life—you're really on the road to hell.

Since love and true friendship fulfill us and give us the meaning of our lives, when you don't have it you reach out through all kinds of compensations—sex, alcohol, materialism, and so forth—to fill the void, and there is no meaning in all of the compensations. Whatever happens to you on your pilgrimage, you must always hope in and believe that God needs you to accomplish His work in you, your transformation into the fullness of your being and to be His child—the only way that this will not come to be is if you decide *to quit!* Remember, the journey is from birth to death, and whether it be a short or long one we have the capacity to face the challenges of loving and being loved—it is a great adventure and yet it is also filled with mystery. You will occasionally get a glimpse of the beauty of your journey, you'll see that from what you experienced as nonmeaning was the very point of opening you to a deeper and richer life. Never "give up"!

Paul VI says that "dialogue is, then, a method of accomplishing the apostolic mission; it is an example of the art of spiritual communication."[16] In meditating on this I saw that it is a method of living out the commandment to love one another. It is, as he says, an art, and like all other arts it requires commitment, discipline, and above all practice! You have to work at it. One of my nephews is a very talented pianist, and his dream has been to become a concert pianist. He works at it, practicing many hours every day, because he wants to perfect his art. We know that anyone who wants to be great in golf, tennis, or whatever must work at it and you might even need an occasional lesson from a pro. It is likewise true if you wish to develop the art of spiritual communication which enables you to enter true friendship, to discover intimacy, and to find the depth and richness that was given to you.

My experience is that many of us find ourselves on a merry-go-round with a lot of other people. Round and round we go. We get so accustomed to the security of being with the crowd that, when someone invites us off the merry-go-round, it is at one moment exciting, adventurous, and yet scary. If we accept the invitation, as soon as we get off the merry-go-round and begin to walk away from it we experience a "pull" to go back. Everyone we know is there, and even though there is no meaning and it is monotonous and boring, it nevertheless has become comfortable, and we know the different horses and the landscape never change. It is secure! In leaving the crowd we will have to embrace insecurity, because this is part and parcel of any pilgrimage, but we will also walk through the valleys, climb the mountains, and experience life as an exciting adventure. Having said yes to the invitation, there is the absolute necessity to let go! When we lift our sails and pull up our anchors, the Holy Spirit will fill our sails with a fresh breeze, and behold the beauty of the sea, the skies, the stars, and life itself. He will carry us through the storms we encounter and we'll eventually enter the harbor of eternal life. Then, and then alone, will you fully know and understand that God was always with you on your journey and you will exclaim, "In trying to live a life of love, all things have worked out unto good!" Meanwhile, we must work at it, we must develop the art of love and friendship.

Paul VI says that there are four major characteristics of this art and that when we live this way, "the union of truth and charity, of understanding and love is achieved."[17] In other words, by developing and perfecting the art of spiritual communication we achieve the integration of truth, charity, understanding, and love. His insights concerning these characteristics are profound and I suggest that you meditate and pray over them—think of your own journey and the impact these have had on you. It is only through this process of reflection and prayer on our journey that we are able to arrive at self-knowledge, which can then become a new starting point.

The first characteristic is *clearness,* and he points out that "this fundamental requirement is enough to enlist our apostolic care to review every angle of our language to guarantee that it be understandable, acceptable, and well-chosen."[18] Language is a vehicle to transmit meaning from within us to another; it embraces verbal, and nonverbal communication. Sensitivity to language is critical and essential to anyone who is committed to a life of dialogue. The meaning within us is usually conveyed through words, and so words play an important role in relationships. Words are not always exact, and often lose their standard meaning and sometimes have different meanings for different people. The transfer of thought and feelings is clearly affected by the differences of sex, age, social, and cultural backgrounds and still other factors which impregnate language with many nuances.

This came home to me personally when the work of the Center for Human Development brought me out of the United States and into other countries and cultures. When I was in England, a priest once asked me what time I wanted to "be knocked up." Well, I was kind of stunned by the question, but found that what he really meant was, What time did I want to get up. Another time someone told me that he was dying for a "fag." In England that means "I'm dying for a cigarette." On the other hand, when I used the term "knickers" to describe the pants that we wore when we were boys, it had a totally different meaning for the English, Scots, and Australians—knickers are women's underwear! Words and phrases do have different meanings and if we care about the transfer of inner meaning it becomes essential to be sensitive in order that our words are understandable, acceptable, and well chosen.

There is another world of language whereby we communicate through touch, signs and symbols—the world of nonverbal communication. Here again one must exercise care that the inner meaning is being communicated lest there be misunderstanding and the loss of dialogue. I often refer to "touch" as a sacrament, in that it must be an external sign of the inward reality, the love we have for one another. In order for this to be true, it becomes absolutely necessary to ask questions which will ensure the honesty of the communication, to ensure the expression of the inner meaning is acceptable, appropriate, and valid. To achieve *clearness* requires a radical commitment to honesty, especially in the area of touch and nonverbal communication.

There is an absolute need to check out with the other what they perceive is the meaning of touch and whether or not it is for them an appropriate vehicle of expression. If you're seeking to be honest and not manipulatively operating out of selfishness and a desire to fulfill your own needs, then you'll be able to ask such questions as What does this say to You? How do you feel? What does it mean to you? How does this affect you? Such questions help to ensure honesty and dialogue. Presuming that the other will likewise strive to be honest with you, then you can be quite sure that you'll find the proper way to express your inner feelings of love and affection in a way that will enhance and deepen the relationship. Touch is one of the most powerful forces we have in communicating love, and everyone needs to touch and be touched. Interestingly, all the Sacraments involve touch, and it is evident from the Scriptures that Christ, our model, was comfortable with touch.

I confess that on my own journey there was a period where I was scared to death of touch, either touching or being touched, since it would call forth emotions and feelings, and sometimes sexual desires. I saw this as negative, destructive, and dangerous, and something that had to be at least controlled, if not killed! Of course such tactics do not work, and it is a good way to become neurotic, leading you into ways that are even far more serious and devastating than touch. I, therefore, had to rediscover this power within me and begin to struggle with finding the way to use this gift and to be able to receive it from others—at times it has been a minefield! You will, no doubt, make mistakes and they are meant to be learning experiences which slowly, but most assuredly, will bring you to the point of being able to exercise the power of touch and to receive it with an inner peace and tranquillity.

The second characteristic of dialogue is "its meekness, the virtue which Christ sets before us to be learned from Him: 'Learn of Me because I am meek and humble of heart.' (Mt. 1:29) . . . the dialogue is not proud, it is not bitter, it is not offensive . . . it is not a command, it is not an imposition. It is peaceful; it avoids violent methods; it is patient; it is generous."[19] Paul VI is describing what we used to call the life of virtue. One can see that "meekness" requires a mutual respect, and avoids anything such as what we call pressure. People who have found great meaning in such movements as Marriage Encounter, Cursillo, Charismatic, to mention only a few, can exert a good deal of pressure to get involved. That pressure, at times, can be in the form of an imposition and one can experience a certain violence and thus be turned off. When individuals do this, with all the goodwill they can muster, there is a lack of peace which is so essential and is always a sign of the presence of the Spirit. I'm not saying that we shouldn't encourage or even endeavor to persuade others to participate in things in which have enriched and helped you on your journey; however, your approach must be patient, generous, and not a command or an imposition, if you wish it to be an encounter in dialogue. I believe that you, more often than not, win "converts" to movements and programs by just being yourself and letting the beauty, power, peace, and meaning that you've found radiate. You'll attract others to want to find what you've found much more quickly than through pressure. There is also a right moment, a right time, and one must exercise the discipline of waiting. When we do wait patiently and in a spirit of meekness, we and others will be enriched because our encounter will be *dialogical.*

The third characteristic is *trust.* Here Paul VI states that "trust promotes confidence and friendship: it binds hearts in mutual adherence to the Good [God] which excludes all self-seeking."[20] For me, this is one of the most profound insights into the problems of our time. If it is true that in our societies today there are many who lack self-confidence, have not found true friendship, have turned to materialism and the use of drugs, alcohol, sex, and other forms of compensation, then according to the insight of Paul VI's it is due to the *fact* that we have lost *trust!* One of the most serious problems arising from the work and research of the Center for Human Development with priests, religious, and laity is *the loss of trust!*

This phenomenon, the failure to trust, surfaced in the early days of the Ministry to Priests Program. On one of those early retreats, a priest approached me and asked if he could see me in private. I said, "Sure, when would you like to see me?" He replied, "If I don't see you now, I'll never see you!" I sensed the urgency and invited him to come to my room. When he sat down he poured out his life and there was certainly plenty of "manure," the faults and failures that arise from the fact that we are wounded human beings, but I didn't hear anything that would have, in my estimation, warranted the urgency that he felt. So I said to him, "Well, so far you've revealed a lot, but there surely must be something more serious for you to have said what you did—I either see you now or never." "No, Vince," he said, "that's it, but I will share with you that I've been carrying this for over eighteen years and there isn't a priest in this diocese that I'd ever dare to share it with." I was shocked and saddened.

Several weeks later I was giving another retreat in a different diocese, and after registering I joined the other priests in the "Happy Hour." Standing next to me was an old priest who had no more than two drinks before the bell rang announcing supper. At the entrance to the dining room we walked down an incline whose floors were well polished and waxed. After picking up my meal in the cafeteria line, I took a seat at one of the many tables and began to enjoy my meal. The last priest to enter was the old priest whom I had been with during the happy hour, and as he came down the incline he slipped and fell. The other priests in the dining room began to laugh and then gave him an applause as he got up and danced a little jig. I left my table and went over to the old priest, who by that time had entered the cafeteria line; his back was to all the others. I put my arm around him and asked him if he was

OK. He turned to me and there were tears flowing down his cheeks, and I said to him, "You got hurt when you fell down?" He replied, "No, Vince, I'm fine, but I'm never coming back to a gathering of priests the rest of my life." I said "You don't mean that," and he then told me that the only reason he had come was because he had heard about my work with priests in the United States and wanted to hear me, but that I didn't understand. "You see, Vince, I have a problem with drinking and sometimes I drink too much, but you were standing with me during happy hour and I only had two drinks. I slipped on the ramp and I am not drunk! But before the night is over it'll be all over the diocese that I was drunk on retreat, and before I get back to my country parish it'll be all over the town that I was drunk on retreat—I can't take it any longer and I'm never coming back!" Before I could say anything, the bishop of the diocese had come up and was standing on his other side and had heard the whole conversation and he told the old priest that he wasn't going to let him go until he promised that he would come back. He went on to tell him that if he were in trouble himself, he could go to the old priest because he would have compassion and understanding and that he wasn't sure he would find that in the others. Finally the old man took his glasses off and wiped his face. The bishop gave him a hug and he finally smiled. I will never forget either of those incidents and assure you that such experiences are not the sole property of priests.

Not long afterward, I returned to my monastery and one day I found myself sitting on the well on top of the hill, one of my spots, pondering the text of Pope Paul and the experiences that I just shared with you. I found myself in the Scriptures and reading the text where Christ invites us to be His friends and He tells us what friendship involves, namely that we are called to reveal and to be able to stand naked with a friend. If we respond to His invitation He tells us that we too must share everything in friendship, and that to love another is very serious business—we must be willing to lay down our life for our friend. As I meditated on this I also recalled that He told us when we had something against another we should leave the altar and go seek out that individual. He did not tell us to go find a priest, a bishop, or, for that matter, anyone other than the individual. He then says that if the encounter with the individual was not productive, then we should return with a friend. Finally, when these two steps have failed we can, and only then, go to the community.

In the early Church these injunctions were seen to be very important, and an offense against them was considered to be a sin against the Holy Spirit—a deadly sin because it can destroy another and is like a cancer that attacks the whole mystical body of Christ, the Church! From these early centuries on through till the thirteenth century we find a rich heritage concerning soul-friendship. It was considered to be a terrible vice to become involved in what we call today "gossip." Even in the Old Testament we're told, "There may be reconciliation with your friend except in the case of upbraiding, reproach, pride, disclosing of secrets or a treacherous wound" (Si 22:27). St. Aelred says, "The revelation of hidden things, that is of secrets, that which nothing is more base, nothing more detestable, leaving no love and no charm between friends, but filling all with the bitterness of indignation and sprinkling all with the venom of hatred and grief. Hence it is written: 'He that discloses the secret of a friend loses his credit . . . To disclose the secrets of a friend leaves no hope to an unhappy soul.' (Sir. 27:17, 27:24) For what is more unfortunate than the man who loses faith

and languishes in despair. The last vice by which friendship is dissolved is treacherous persecution, which is nothing other than secret detraction. A treacherous blow indeed, it is the death-dealing blow of the serpent and the
asp. 'If a serpent bite in silence,' says Solomon, 'he is no
better who backbites secretly.' (Eccles. 10:11) Therefore,
should you discover anyone habituated to these vices, you
ought to avoid him . . . Let us renounce slander, the
avenger of which is God."[21]

The words of Cardinal Newman also ring clear when he
said that the reason for a lack of sanctity in his time was
because people could no longer trust the secrets of their
hearts with one another. And, in our own times the words
of Paul VI articulate clearly and profoundly that it is *trust*
which fosters self-confidence and friendship, and that
only in friendship are our hearts bound up in God, which
in turn prevents all self-seeking. According to Christ, the
true meaning of life is found only in true, spiritual friendship—love of one another! When you haven't found a soul-
friend you find yourself in the midst of compensations:
materialism, sex, alcohol, drugs, and so forth. Since these
become compensations for the lack of true meaning, we
find them to be, ultimately, empty and void of meaning.

I could relate many examples of people who have been
devastated by gossip, and which we accept in our society
today just as we accept the fact that we need to breathe
air to live! Furthermore, "rumors" are just as destructive.
This present atmosphere poisons the environment that is
so necessary for true friendship to flourish. Each of us can
do something about it if we were to take heed of Christ's
injunction. I assure you that if the next time someone
comes to you with a story about another person and you
ask them if they have gone to that person and they respond in the negative, then suggest that they first go to

the person and, if that doesn't work out, offer to go with them. After a couple of times the word will go out that you won't tolerate gossip or rumors. If each of us were to take this kind of gospel stand, we would put a serious dent into this insidious vice, if not kill it! If you have ever experienced this in your own journey then you know the pain, hurt, and the heroic effort involved in getting up and giving your trust to another.

It's surprising that what the mystics considered lesser faults and failures that flow from our woundedness we consider the major sins, and what they saw as deadly we have come to consider to be the minor vices. Participating in gossip and spreading stories, true or false, are sins against the Holy Spirit and attack the very body of Christ: the individual member, the community—the Mystical Body of Christ!

St. James points out in a very vivid way how terrible are the consequences of gossip and rumors when he says:

> Once we put a bit in the horse's mouth, to make it do what we want, we have the whole animal under our control. Or think of ships: no matter how big they are, even if a gale is driving them, they are directed by a tiny rudder wherever the whim of the helmsman decides. So the tongue is only a tiny part of the body, but its boasts are great. Think how small a flame can set fire to a huge forest; The tongue is a flame too. Among all the parts of the body, the tongue is a whole wicked world: it infects the whole body; catching fire itself from hell, it sets fire to the whole wheel of creation. Wild animals and birds, reptiles and fish of every kind can all be tamed, and have been tamed, by humans; but nobody can tame the tongue—it is a pest that will not keep still, full of deadly poison. We use it to bless

the Lord and Father, but we also use it to curse people who are made in God's image: the blessing and curse come out of the same mouth. My brothers, this must be wrong. (Jm 3:3–10)

Brothers, do not slander one another. Anyone who slanders a brother, or condemns one, is speaking against the Law and condemning the Law. But if you condemn the Law, you have ceased to be subject to it and become a judge over it. There is only one lawgiver and he is the only judge and has the power to save or to destroy. Who are you to give a verdict on your neighbour? (Jm 4:11–12)

And he sums it all up when he states: "Nobody who fails to keep a tight rein on the tongue can claim to be religious; this is mere self-deception; that person's religion is worthless" (Jm 1:26).

It is indeed a major challenge to embrace the necessary discipline to control our tongues and refuse to participate in gossip and rumors. It is, as I've already said, one of the most destructive things I've encountered. We know the damage and the incredible agony we experience when something we've shared or done, which we entrusted to another, has been betrayed. Whom do we then turn to in order to reveal our inner struggles? Whom shall we now trust? This destructive force, gossip and rumors, cries out to the Christian community for the need to bring it to an end!

The fourth characteristic is *prudence.* St. Thomas Aquinas says that this virtue is the queen of all the virtues. It is fascinating to see how Paul VI uses it in the context of dialogue. He says that prudence "esteems highly the psychological and moral circumstances of the listener

(cf. Mt. 7:6), whether he be a child, uneducated, unpre-
pared, defiant, hostile; prudence strives to learn the sensitivities of the hearer and requires that we adapt ourselves
and the manner of presentation in a reasonable way lest
we be displeasing and incomprehensible."[22] Dialogue
thus requires that we adapt ourselves to the sensitivities of
the other, that we pay attention to where they are and
where they're coming from. To know the psychological
and moral circumstances of the other requires that we
listen to each other. I must first be tuned in to myself,
capable of listening to my own heart and in touch with my
own self-knowledge. I can then listen to the heart of another and adapt myself when necessary. Once again you
can see the stress on and the importance of self-knowledge, and why the mystics maintain we must be grounded
in humility.

From these four characteristics of the art of spiritual
communication, true dialogue, one begins to wonder how
to bring it into the mainstream of our daily lives. "Many,
indeed are the forms that dialogue of salvation can take. It
adapts itself to the needs of a concrete situation, it chooses
the appropriate means, it does not bind itself to ineffec-
tual theories and does not cling to hard and fast forms
when these have lost their power to speak to men and
move them. The question is of great importance, for it
concerns the relation of the Church's mission to the lives
of men in a given time and place, in a given culture and
social setting."[23] Each of us is given a mission, that of
announcing and spreading the Good News of Christ. Each
one has the opportunity of touching the lives of those we
come in contact with, and we can touch them for better or
for worse. It depends on whether we are trying to love
one another, trying to be open to the gift of true friendship, and willing to walk with one another as wounded

pilgrims on a journey, needing the support and encouragement of one another.

In the Introduction I noted that in our society most people seem to be in the stage of "role conformity and role expectation"—they endeavor to live their lives based on their perceived understanding of their role and the expectations of others. That role-playing can be on the part of a mother, father, doctor, priest, minister, bishop, head of a corporation, and so on. Once you assume or are given a position in society, there is an image of what that means and entails. Here it becomes possible to begin to play the role and not to be true to ourselves. Paul VI places before us an alternative to role-playing when he says: "In the very act of trying to make ourselves pastors, fathers, and teachers . . . we must make ourselves brothers."[24] Hence, if you assume any of these possible roles you must first be willing to be as brother, as sister. You must be willing to be you! The mask, the role, will prevent you from becoming a brother or a sister.

When I first reflected on the above, it brought to mind the research that was going on concerning integration, internalization, and assimilation of content in the classroom. The research indicated that if I remain in the role of professor and the student remains in his/her role, then all we have is the transmission of facts, figures, and data. Integration and internalization become rare, and students tend to regurgitate what has been given to them. It is only when I'm willing to come from around the podium and be Vincent Dwyer, and the students are able to be themselves, do we have the possibility of integration and internalization. Hence, the need to get out of the roles and to be ourselves. Let me illustrate this with several stories that had an impact on my grasp of the importance of this. Perhaps it will resonate with your experiences.

Years ago I was giving the Center's report, which is a part of our Ministry to Priests Program, to the Diocese of Manchester, New Hampshire. During one of the breaks an old priest approached me and said, "You must be Kevin and Norma's boy!" I was startled; I didn't know the priest and yet he was indicating that he knew my parents. My parents had grown up in Nashua, New Hampshire, and it turned out that the priest had been a childhood friend to both of them. He took me aside and when we sat down he proceeded to tell me stories about my parents, especially my father. After each story he would ask me, "Did they ever tell you that?" Of course, I replied in the negative. We were running out of time and he concluded by saying, "I know one story your father must have told you; the time when we were down at your grandfather's farm and we got into his homemade beer and had too much—now he told you that one?" When I said no, he commented on how sad it was that they had never told me any of those stories. I remember saying to him, "Father, it's not just sad, it's tragic that my parents were part of a culture that told them to stay in their roles and not share their own faults, mistakes, successes."

Right after that I went home and, while searching for something, I opened an old sea chest and I found a packet of letters written to my mother when she was at Skidmore College. The packet had a bow on it and, since my mother had been dead for many years, I presumed her permission to take a peek. The first letter I opened was a love letter—it was fascinating, page after page, but when I got to the end it was signed, Love John! I said to myself, "That's not the ole man!" There were others and each one was signed by some other name, and I sat there and said to myself, "Mom ran around!" It was a little naive, to say the least, that I would think that my mother never went out with anyone other than Dad, but I wished she had been able to share that part of her life with me. I believe that, if they had been able to share their own stories of their journeys, their struggles, it would have invited me to share my own with them. I too began to play the role and shared only what they expected from me. Society and the cultural impact had prevented us from moving beyond the relationship of parent to son and to become friends.

One summer I borrowed my brother's sailboat and went sailing in the Cape Cod area of Massachusetts. One of my nephews along with one of his friends joined me with another friend who was a priest. We anchored at Provincetown the first night, and after supper we were sitting up topside when my nephew started to share some heavy things. I asked him if he had shared them with his father and he said, "No!" I then asked if he had told his mother, and again he replied in the negative. I then asked him if it was because I was a priest that he felt so easy in sharing his ups and downs. "Oh, no! All of us kids feel that we can talk to you about anything, because you have always told us about your own struggles—how you got kicked out of school, and Gramps also told us a lot of other stories about you, so we feel that we can tell you anything." I then said to him, "Oh! You don't think your parents would be able to understand what you're going through?" "No, they wouldn't understand," he said. I then proceeded to tell him some stories, especially about his father, my brother. After each story he'd say, "I don't believe that!" "Well, when we get home, you ask your father," I replied.

After sailing to Martha's Vineyard and Nantucket we returned home, and during this time I had forgotten all about our conversation in Provincetown. When we arrived home we were unloading the boat before taking it to the mooring, and my nephew began to relate my stories to his father concerning his younger years. Needless to say, I was in trouble and my brother said, "That's the problem with you priests, you don't know how hard it is to raise kids these days. We don't need you telling them any stories!" After mooring the boat, I went into his home where they were having a family get-together. He came over to me and apologized. He then said that he didn't want to loose his son and found it difficult to understand how his son could embrace me and share with me whatever he wanted. He missed that gift in their relationship and asked me to help him. I then quoted Paul VI and suggested that it might be time for him to become a brother, too. "I'm his father, not his brother," he replied. I went on to encourage him to open himself to the possibility of becoming a brother, a friend. This meant that he had to be open to sharing with his son, his own struggles in order that his son might relate to him in a new way. I told him that it wasn't something that required him to sit down and tell him everything about his life, but that he needed to share his own story at the right moment, and that the dialogue would have its own rhythm.

Several months passed and he called me one evening to inform me that he wasn't sure about my advice. He then shared with me that his son had come home one night and asked him if he wanted to hear a joke. My brother put down the newspaper and said "Sure!" His son proceeded to tell him an off-color joke. He said to me, "Can you imagine what would have happened to us if we ever did that with Dad?" "Yes," I said, "I can hear him yelling and asking us whom we were hanging around with and con-

cluding by saying, 'You're grounded!' " "Exactly," my
brother said, "and it was as if he were on one side of me
telling me to put him in his place, and you were on the
other side telling me to be myself, to be a brother."
"Well," I said, "what did you do?" "It was funny, so I
laughed," my brother replied. "That's great," I said. "No!
He went on to tell me another worse one!" Alas, it is
indeed risky in trying to be a brother, a friend.

Later on my nephew went off to the university and
during his first year he wrote me a letter telling me that
he thought he might flunk out and felt that he had let me
down and his parents also. I called him and told him that I
didn't care whether he stayed there or not, but I did care,
very much, that he knew that I loved him as he was,
believed in him, and would do anything I could do to
support and help him. I then asked him if he wanted me
to talk to his father. He said that he'd appreciate that very
much. I called my brother, and he was aware of his son's
difficulties. I suggested that it would be great if he would
invite his son to lunch and talk with him. He agreed and I
then suggested that it would be a great opportunity for
him to share his own experience in his first year at college.
There was dead silence at the other end and so I asked
him if he was still there. "Yes, I'm here," he said. In his first
year at college he had some academic difficulties which
had forced him to change majors, not to mention the
wrath of my father. He did have lunch with his son, and
told him that he and his mother felt the same as I did—
that they loved him, just as he was. He then went on to
share with him his difficulties in his first year at college
and how he had changed majors but that it had merely
opened up new doors for him in an area that had later
provided him with success. "So," he said to his son, "you

see things do work out, and they will work out for you because you're a great guy!" When they stood up at the end of lunch in the Executive Dining Room, his son embraced his father and thanked him. Upon returning to the university, he then wrote me a letter and told me that it was the first time that he had ever thought that he and his father could become friends! Behold the incredible power and beauty that deeply touched both of them in and through sharing which changed their relationship from one of roles to one of friendship. Each of us has the opportunity of stepping aside from roles we assume, or which others try to place us in, and strive to live a life of dialogue —loving one another, just as we are!

The life of dialogue, of true friendship and love, is the path to deep, inner meaning. It offers each of us a way of living out our commitment to follow Christ. It does require a commitment. And like other commitments we must aim to put everything into it, if we ever hope to experience the fruits that always flow from our commitments. When one only invests 95 percent, or even 99 percent, there remains a part of us that is not committed and that part will slowly destroy the commitment.

"It is a cause of joy and comfort to see that such a dialogue is already in existence in the Church and in the areas which surround it. The Church today is more than ever alive. But it seems good to consider that everything still remains to be done; the work begins today and never comes to an end. This is the law of our temporal, earthly pilgrimage."[25] Thus, as Paul VI says, we must each take up the challenge of dialogue and begin anew each day, for it offers us the way of truly loving one another, of following the Lord!

"THE WINDS OF GOD'S GRACE ARE ALWAYS BLOWING, BUT WE MUST MAKE AN EFFORT TO RAISE OUR SAILS."

REFLECTIONS

1. Identify a time when you made a radical decision concerning the direction of your life, an either/or decision. What were the events leading to such a decision? How did you come to make it?

2. Identify the times when you have attached "strings" to a gift of your love and friendship. What specific discipline is required by you to leave people "free"?

3. Have you ever confided in someone, shared yourself, and found yourself betrayed? How did you feel? What can you do in your own environment to put a stop to "gossip and rumors"?

SUGGESTED READINGS

1. Pope Paul VI. *Paths of the Church [Ecclesiam Suam]*. Paulist Press, 1964.

2. Martin Buber. *I and Thou*. Charles Scribner's, Sons, 1958.

3. Raoul Howe. *The Miracle of Dialogue*. Seabury Press, 1963.

4. Martin E. Marty. *Friendship*. Argus Communications, 1980.

CHAPTER V

THE WOUNDED PILGRIM

To live a life of dialogue requires effort, perseverance, and a willingness to begin anew each day. This, it seems to me, presupposes a deep commitment to a "way" of life. Dialogue, as we have discussed it, is the relationship that exists between an I and a Thou, and also it determines the communication. The person who has "opted" for a life of dialogue has chosen a way that is open to all. No one is excluded, Martin Buber says; "the life of dialogue is no privilege of intellectual activity like dialectic. It does not begin in the upper story of humanity. It begins no higher than where humanity begins. There are no gifted and ungifted here, only those who give themselves and those who withhold themselves. And he who gives himself . . . does not know that he has it in himself . . . he will just find it, "and finding, be amazed."[1]

To enter dialogue, a true friendship, one must be trying to be totally present, listening beyond words and to the heart of another, being both a teacher and a learner, able to give and to receive love, and above all, one who can forgive, be forgiven, heal and be healed in and through the other. The dialogical life cannot be lived without a basic awareness that we have been created to relate, that only in loving one another do we find ultimate meaning.

As I've pointed out, dialogue is not merely conversation, nor is it a friendly chat; it is much more. The opposite is "monologue," and Buber says that "the 'Eros of monologue' has many varieties: there a lover stamps around and is in love only with his passion. . . . There one is enjoying the adventure of his own fascinating effect. There one is gazing enraptured at the spectacle of his own supposed surrender. There one is collecting excitement. There one is displaying his 'power' . . . there one is delighting to exist simultaneously as himself and as an idol very unlike himself . . . and so on and on—all the manifold monologists with their mirrors, in the apartment of the most intimate dialogue! . . . They are all beating the air."[2]

Paul Tournier says, "The whole difference between an individual and a person is that the individual associates, whereas the person communicates."[3] The more that you refuse to communicate, to enter dialogue, the life of relatedness which leads to soul-friendship, the more you sink into the monological world where there is no meaning and into a life of compensation! The monological person is totally concerned with self. He/she refuses to respond as a whole person, and merely remains physically present. Such persons tend to lead others to an expectation, one which they are unwilling to follow through on. They use people as things and manipulate them to serve and confirm themselves. It is obvious that here lies what we might call "true sin," when we deal with others only in terms of their function or usefulness—persons become objects. Buber puts this in a very powerful way when he says, "Love without dialogue, without real outgoing to the other, reaching to the other, and accompanying with the other, the love remaining with itself . . . this is called Lucifer."[4]

The Scriptures tell us that we are created to the image and likeness of God, that we are born with original sin, we are wounded pilgrims on a journey to the Father, Who is Love. Each of us is created to love and be loved, but the ideal is the perfection of love. I must point out that perfection is also a gift, and one that usually is the product of a life of trying to follow Christ, trying to love one another. Perfection of virtue, of a chosen state of life and, for that matter, any aspect of our lives is rarely, if ever, given or achieved in an instant—it is the work of a lifetime.

At birth we are totally dependent for all our needs, and one of the most significant needs is to be touched. Research indicates that frustrations of the need to be touched and cared for causes anxieties and tensions which can develop into psychosomatic disorders, if not into neuroses. Furthermore, it is clear also from the massive amount of research undertaken in this area that the first six years of our life are critical in establishing our ability to love and be loved. That's kind of scary. Very few of us were born into a family with perfect mothers and fathers, and within an environment that was ideal. Thus, we struggle on our own journey, just as our parents before us. There was only one person who was born perfect: Jesus Christ! The rest of us must face the fact that we have all kinds of needs, some of which are sought after in ways that are not from love, but rather from selfishness. So, we are mixtures of both good and evil.

There is a basic disorientation which becomes ours and we had nothing to go with it—it is a given! As the author of *The Cloud* reminds us, "we will never be entirely free in this life, no matter how holy we become."[5] Since this woundedness is a given, then we must come to embrace it, accept it, and deal with it. You can get yourself into a quagmire, however, if you fail to embrace another given, the unconditional love of God. His love embraces you, as you are: in your imperfections, sinfulness, and so forth— He has revealed this incredible love in and through His Son, Jesus Christ, who became a human person, just like us except for that basic disorientation which we call original sin. This love was expressed in the fullest possible way when He died for each of us on the Cross. He took upon Himself all of our faults, failures, sins, and made them His own so that you and I could be free. Free to live as children of God.

I have come to a conviction, from my own journey and in walking with others, that the real and perhaps, only significant "crisis" in life is failing to accept and embrace the totality of the redemptive act of Christ in my own personal life. He has already embraced us, even those very areas that we so dislike about ourselves. This unconditional love is a given, the gift of His unconditional love. Because we are wounded, our journeys will include failures, faults, and sins. We, like St. Paul, begin to cry out from our hearts that the things that we really want to do, and the way we want to live, are not done, not lived out. And, likewise, at times those things that I do, and the way that I live, run counter to all I aspire to. Paul describes this struggle between his love of Christ and desire to live out His commandments and the reality of not achieving this goal as a direct result of "sin that lives in me" (cf. Letter of Paul to the Church in Rome, 7:14–25). Our given woundedness is indeed a mystery. It is also reality, and the struggle to love and be loved, to taste that unconditional love, which has also been a given, are the very ingredients of life. The integration, assimilation, and internalization of the Good News is a work of a lifetime and each of us is destined to reach the peak of the mountain where everything comes together all because we tried to follow Him. That transformation into the fullness of the life of Christ requires our involvement, but it is mainly the work of the Holy Spirit.

From birth we reach out for affirmation, acceptance, security; we desire to know and be known, to love and be loved, and there is within us an urgency to fulfill the need to be related and to communicate. Many times we fail; fail to be dialogical, fail in the bonds of love and friendship. Yet these failures, and even sins, are invitations to learn and grow, and although they can be painful, they can become steps on the staircase to perfect union with God.

In our rich tradition we are told over and over again that the Christian life essentially is a growth into freedom and the perfection of friendship, friendship with one another and with God. Aelred identifies and unifies the two in telling us that "God is friendship and that one who dwells in friendship dwells in God and God in him."[6] Hence, friendship and love are the very foundations of the Christian life, and one's openness to and experience of these brings meaning and fulfillment. The refusal to receive love, when coupled with a refusal to give love, will inevitably bring death to the soul. The demands and the seriousness of love is well expressed in the currently popular book *The Little Prince:* "When you tame someone, you become responsible forever." Thus, every time I have communicated my love to another, I have made a commitment, forever! I have said that I'll attempt always to respond to the best of my ability to the other, with all that I am and have—without boundaries or limitations.

We live in a world today in which the term "love" is found in songs, poetry, films, plays, and countless other forms. It seems indicative of the hunger of people to find love and friendship, a need that we acquire at the moment of our birth. As we reach out to others to discover and experience love, we will inevitably encounter pain, self-doubt, mistakes, and failures that arise from our inability to pull it off, or the inability of others to respond. There are on the journey broken relationships that began with the hope of intimacy, friendship, and commitment, only to fall apart. Like the tide, the sea ebbs, and we find ourselves on the sand, left behind, vulnerable and tempted: to pull out, to quit! The alternative to quitting is to pick yourself up, embrace your cross, and let Him help you. The mystics and saints encourage us in such situations to "run" to Him, and in running to Him with our hurts, faults, sins, and failures, we experience acceptance, forgiveness, and healing. The difficulty is in believing and in trusting Him.

The principles of dialogue and friendship must come into play in every relationship that we enter. We first create an environment of invitation, leaving others free to accept or reject our invitation to relationship. When someone does respond, then we have the beginning of a process that can lead to the depths of intimacy and love and likewise it can lead nowhere but to the hurts and pain we have discussed. Every relationship begins with a desire to know one another and involves a mutual sharing which requires a listening heart. There is a flow which the Holy Spirit guides, and it is essential to listen to the invitation of one another and not give way to our needs. When our needs to know and be known become the driving force, then we more often than not leave the flow, the rhythm of dialogue, and we find ourselves high and dry— the relationship falls apart. The temptation to build a wall around ourselves almost always follows on this, a temptation that must not be given into.

When affirmation, acceptance, and love are given, it is essential to reflect on these positive elements of our journey and to internalize them. In failing to do this, we will continue to suffer from poor self-image. I'm always amazed, within the context of my own family, that some of my nephews and nieces will identify their lack of a positive self-concept with the lack of affirmation, acceptance, and love on the part of their parents and the rest of us. However, when I've had the opportunity to talk with them about this we have found that they have missed the positive things on their journey and hence the poor self-image. There was a song during World War II which I think should become the theme song for all of us: "Accent-tchu-ate the Positive"! God is continually trying to communicate His unconditional love. It is, however, communicated in and through the events of our journey, and especially through people. We often "miss" this great *gift* because we assume it will come from a particular source or person while all the time missing it because God has chosen to give it to us through another.

As relationships develop, it's possible to reach a "plateau": it doesn't involve us in the depth and intimacy that we hunger for. There are many today who want and try to produce intimacy at whatever cost, and no doubt this reflects our society with our expectation to have everything in an instant: fast food, instant relief of headaches, instant breakfast, and so forth. If you try to produce intimacy, like an instant breakfast, then you can be absolutely sure that you're going to be without any breakfast. Intimacy is a *gift* and cannot be forced!

It takes great patience and prudence to allow another to let down the walls. There is a need for respect and for allowing individual freedom. Those relationships that never go beyond a plateau are painful, and yet you can never be sure that at some point in time they will grow deeper, and so one must wait. In that waiting period you must maintain an environment of openness, care, warmth, and readiness to respond. In my own journey there have been times when years passed before a relationship moved to a new level.

Loving another and being loved is a process that opens us to peak experiences and transcendence. It also poses difficulties, love rarely stays on an intellectual level but involves our emotions and passions, and can call forth our sexual drives. In the old days we were often encouraged to "love, intellectually"! This was indeed a safe doctrine, and it ensured that those kinds of relationships would always be safe and secure from faults, failures, or sin. Of course, there is also little connection with another when we tell them "I'm in love with your intellect!" As the kids today would say, "It doesn't turn me on!" It might have been safe, but it was not real!

One's emotions, feelings, and even passions inevitably enter into play, and this is a normal development in a relationship that is calling us into the bonds of love and friendship. Another injunction from the past was that we should put strict controls on this area, if not to stifle it completely. Run five miles, or take a cold shower, was the recommended activity to diminish or kill this sudden flow of energy and power. Needless to say, try whatever you like, but you'll not succeed in suppressing these feelings and emotions. God created us with them and we must learn to use them in a positive and constructive way within those relationships that call us to friendship and love.

This sexual drive has been given to us by God, and is a beautiful and powerful *gift!* It is not ugly or dirty even though there are those who might view sex in this way. In loving relationships one would normally experience some sexual feelings, and it is a challenging task to integrate in a wholesome way this aspect of the relationship. One can run from it, break off a relationship in which you experience this area of self, but you can be sure that it will surface again and again. We must begin to face the need to become comfortable with our sexuality and to realize that sexual expression is a beautiful *gift,* and yet not necessary in achieving intimacy or soul-friendship.

The gift of sexuality is powerful and can be misused to manipulate and treat other persons as objects. Sin enters where there is no commitment, no dialogue, a lack of honesty and friendship. There is only *you* and the *object* of your desire.

There are differing views of how and when our sexual identity is established. For some it is seen as a choice which we made and have the power to change. Others, in the light of current research, hold that our sexual identity is well established in the first few years of our life when we know little, if anything, about sex, let alone in choosing our sexual identity. No doubt the debate will continue, however; what is important is that we are able to finally embrace ourselves, as we are! It is only in self-acceptance, as St. Teresa of Ávila and other mystics tell us, that we can then turn to God for the help we need in living out our particular state in life. The same challenge to living out the principles of dialogue and the life of spiritual friendship must be faced whether one's sexual orientation is heterosexual, homosexual, or bisexual. Once again it needs to be stated that true meaning, offered to us in and through following Christ, is found only in the intimacy of a soul-friendship. Sexual expression can indeed be powerful, beautiful, and a sign of unity; nevertheless, it is not essential to finding true meaning. This is verified over and over again in marriage, where, for numerous reasons, the couple are not able to express their love and intimacy in a sexual way. Married persons have shared with me that when sexual expression of their relationship was denied due to health problems, they nevertheless found other ways to express their intimacy because they were soul-friends!

The more we open ourselves to love and soul-friend-ship, the greater the possibility of our total involvement in such relationships, calling forth our whole being. Inevitably there arises in such relationships the desire to express our affection and care. The expression of affection involves touch, and this can literally take us quickly into forms of expression which can or cannot be true expressions of spiritual friendship and love. We are dealing with a very powerful force. In order to find the proper expression of touch in each relationship, since no two relationships are the same, we must ask questions to ensure that the touch is a true and acceptable expression of our affection. When touch is used in a sacramental way, as I said earlier, it produces fruit: inner peace, a growth in self-acceptance, a deeper awareness of one's lovableness and tranquillity—these are signs of the presence of the Holy Spirit. On the other hand, if we discover that we really don't want to ask any questions involving the meaning of touch, and in the wake of touch we experience tension, anxieties, a loss of self-esteem and above all a lack of inner peace, then you can be sure that the touch and affection you're involved in is taking you down the wrong path and you're heading for a disaster. A disaster, because every time we violate true love we inflict an injury, not only on the other, but also on ourselves—the personhood of both is diminished! The force and power of affection when coupled with touch can put us on a fast roller coaster

which can take us at a fast speed where, in fact, we actually do not want to go. Some, therefore, have concluded
that the obvious way to deal with this force is to suppress
it, kill it, lock it up, and throw the key away! That might be
considered safe, but it is, in reality, death! Touch, can be
considered under the umbrella of the art of spiritual communication, and therefore we must work at it, develop
the art to touch and be touched with honesty. The alternative is to remove yourself from growth and withdraw
into your safe little world where you won't make any
mistakes, you won't love, you won't fall—no, you'll live in
your pride, conceit, self-centeredness; compensating in a
million different ways that seem more acceptable, but
nevertheless have the same devastating result, in that life
will pass by and you'll never have lived, because you
wouldn't take the risk to love or be loved. It is indeed risky
and, yet, is there another way? Can you use whatever
cliché or pious saying you can find to justify not coming to
grips with this powerful force of the totality of love, of
communicating that which you have received from God
—given not to be buried but to touch others and bring
them the love He gave you to give away?

The Commandments, and the moral teachings of the
Church, are placed before you over and over again, in
many different forums, and it is not the task at hand to
restate them. The task we face, it seems to me, is to consider some ways of dealing with your failures and sins in a
constructive way. We need to deal with the fact that we
are wounded and we do fall down, fail to live out our
cherished ideals. Like the old saying, "There is many a slip
between our ideals and values and life as it is concretely
lived."

Each of us, on our journey, make commitments based
on ideals and values and as we endeavor to live them out.

Even with the highest and best intentions, we do sometimes fail. The *gift* of a vocation, whether it be marriage, priesthood, religious life, or the single state, is indeed a grace that moves us to accept the responsibilities of our vocation. One must never forget, though, that the fullness of the gift is not usually given on the day that we respond to the call of our vocation. We do indeed receive the gift, but the bestowal of the perfection of the gift is His work, and He gives it in His own time and in His way. Meanwhile, we must continue striving to follow Him and deal in a constructive way with any failures we encounter on the road to soul-friendship and love of one another.

The mystics and saints continually warn us concerning the seriousness of the sin of pride. Pride can be deeply rooted within us, and in order to uproot this terrible sin and major obstacle to growth in the spiritual life, we have to risk falling. However, in order to get at the roots of pride, many of the spiritual authors indicate that God will allow us to fall in areas that will lead us to feel ashamed of ourselves. When you fall, fail to live up to the Gospel values, and if your immediate reaction is "How could I ever have done that" or "What would other people think of me if they knew this," you can be certain that the fault or failure that you've encountered is a direct attack on your real problem, which is pride! If you were grounded in humility, your reaction to failure would be "What else is new?" "I can't make it on my own—I need to be forgiven and healed." And thus from failure you would find yourself turning to God, directly and often indirectly through another. Your woundedness would provide you the opportunity to seek forgiveness, and allow another to exercise the power we've been given to forgive one another; in and through that experience, we taste the forgiveness, acceptance, and love of God. Something far greater can happen in embracing our failures, whatever they may be, and dealing with them in a constructive way, rather than projecting them on to others or to circumstances—for example, "I was drinking too much," "I was feeling down," and other such statements which seemingly remove us from responsibility.

Most of our faults and failures, especially in the area of sexuality, alcohol, and overindulgence, flow directly from our "given" woundedness. They can absorb our attention and we can set out on every conceivable program to rid ourselves of them, but until we reach a point of seeing them as signs to something far more serious, then we miss the boat. As I indicated above, the far more serious problem we face is pride! Proud persons do not reach out to seek forgiveness, nor are they filled with honest contrition and sorrow for any hurts they may have inflicted on another through their failure. Quite the contrary, they spend their time in self-righteousness, and quickly resume their roles of judges on the behavior of others. The "wounded" will be saved, they will be forgiven, and healed—Christ came for them! The "proud and conceited" walk a dangerous path, and only through faults and failures do they have the possibility of turning to God. Whatever faults, failures, and sins you fall into on your journey, you can rise from them, learn, grow, and discover mercy, forgiveness, self-acceptance, and the ability to love yourself, as you are, in and through true friends whom you turn to, who provide you with a taste and experience of the incredible, unconditional love of God!

A woman called me one evening. She and her family were very close to me, and I've always felt a part of their family. She was crying. She finally was able to share with me what was causing so much pain. Her husband had just come home and confessed that he had been having an affair. Her immediate reaction, arising from the pain and feeling of utter betrayal, was to leave him—get a divorce! During the conversation I asked her what she thought the revelation said to her, since he could have kept it a secret and never revealed it. After a pause, she said that he must have trusted her, trusted her love for him, and believed that somehow she would forgive him. I then asked her if she had ever before experienced a situation or circumstance in which he had stood so "naked," so in need of her understanding, compassion, and forgiveness? She confided that he had never expressed such a radical need for her, and in fact had always been very self-assured and self-reliant. I asked her to consider that what had happened could well have been necessary for them to really enter the depths of soul-friendship, where they could share anything and know that the other would always be there. She had the power to forgive him, and to begin again on a radically new level of communication, honesty, and love of each other. I encouraged her to embrace him in his frailty and forgive him, and stressed to her how much he needed her. She returned home to him and did embrace him, in all of his weakness, and forgave him. Several years later, I was visiting the family, and she said jokingly, "Well, Vince, I'm ready for him to have another affair!" When I asked her "How come," she shared that the whole thing had opened them to true friendship, that they had never been so happy with each other, and she concluded by saying, "Vince, it transcends any kind of honeymoon . . . we've become *friends!*"

Not all experiences of our woundedness end that way, but we do have the power, each one of us, to turn our failures into a growth toward deeper intimacy where we can stand "naked" and come to know that a friend can embrace us, just as we are! The things that we most dislike about ourselves, when known, can be accepted. The beauty and also the warts make us who we are and whenever we experience another person loving us, as we are, it is a precious *gift!* That *gift* is a taste of His unconditional love for us and it is an essential experience on the journey, if you're going to continue climbing the mountain to soul-friendship, to love of one another, to God!

When you become involved in relationships that call forth your inner gift of loving and receiving love in return, there is always the risk that you'll go beyond the proper limits and thus fail in your commitments. I've always experienced a great compassion for people who are trying to love, and who encounter their woundedness and inability to always and everywhere act in perfect conformity to their values and the Gospel values. However, I find it very difficult to deal with persons who use others as objects. I recall one time when a gentleman came to me and shared that he went regularly to a house of prostitution and then said, "Well, you understand, Father—it's just being normal!" I told him I didn't see anything "normal" about it at all. In fact, I saw it as being detestable in using another person as an object. I then asked him what he thought of people who went to gay bars to pick up someone? He exploded with all kinds of abusive language describing homosexuals. I said, "What's the difference? You use women, and they use men." I went on to try and point out to him that all promiscuous behavior is deadly. He concluded by saying, "But I tip well!" . . . I just wanted to vomit!

As I've said before, almost all growth takes place as a result of mistakes, making bad choices and bad decisions. Yet, these can become a reservoir from which we can develop warning signals in the future—warning us of the potholes and side roads that we have already fallen into.

We have the ability to learn from our mistakes and hope-fully to make new ones, rather than continue to make the same ones. However, in order to learn, one must reflect and pray, and it can be very beneficial to share our jour-ney with a trusted friend, a confidant, a soul-friend.

Whenever we share our struggles with another and the struggle involves another person, we need to be very careful not to reveal the name of the other whom we are involved with. We must *always* seek the permission of the other before revealing that person's identity. Whatever has taken place between you and another is a mutual revelation that is sacred, and any violation of that sacred-ness is disastrous! Often, people will come to me and share some difficulty that they're experiencing in a particular relationship and, before you know it, they have revealed who the other person is. I immediately ask them if they have the permission of the other, and almost always they'll admit that they don't. When I go on to ask them how they think the other person might feel if they knew that their identity had been revealed, especially if I know the other person, they'll respond by telling me that they think the other would be crushed! You can talk to me about anything you choose, and you can seek advice from others, but you have no right to reveal, without permis-sion, the name of the other person involved. Everything that is shared and experienced in a relationship is sacred to that relationship.

I have known and directed many people on the jour-ney, and I assure you that there is a great deal of pain, hurt, and loss of trust that is directly due to the betrayal of confidences and secrets shared within the context of a relationship. I now understand why Aelred maintained that this fault was indeed the most wretched thing a Christian could do. It is, in my estimation, more destructive and far worse than any failure or faults in the area of sexuality, alcohol, drugs, or other possible compensations that flow from our human frailty and woundedness. It is deadly because it crushes hope and trust within people; it attacks the very life of community. When Paul VI pointed out the consequences of the loss of trust as being poor self-concept, the loss of friendship, and a falling away to materialism and a life of compensations, you need only to look at your own journey and then look around you—it is self-evident!

Sometime ago a priest friend called me and shared some difficulty he was facing, which was quite serious. He came to grips with what he had to do, and that involved getting some professional help. There were only three of us with whom he shared his problem and the fact that he was going to seek the necessary professional help to work it through. Shortly afterward, I had to make a trip to Europe and went to Rome for a meeting. While in Rome, I ran into another priest who was from the same diocese and immediately he asked me if I knew that the priest had left the diocese for help. I asked him where he had heard that, and he told me that it was all over the diocese. Devastating, crushing—it's impossible to find words adequate to describe the effects of "gossip and rumors"! I find it hard to believe, but it happens more often than I'd want to mention, not just with priests, but with everyone.

In the days when I grew up there were things in the community that remained secret. There seemed to be an unspoken awareness of the sacredness of trust. This was especially true of any faults or weaknesses that were in the family, or those that lived in the neighborhood, or for that matter, in the local parish—they remained within and you'd have a hard time to find any significant violations. Today, that seems to be gone. We seem to be driven to get to the nearest phone and blurt out the latest piece of "garbage" we have fallen onto. I pray every day that once again we will restore that environment of trust and confidentiality. The Shepherds of the Church need to challenge us to rebuild this environment of trust and love where we can share, grow, be forgiven, and healed. The disease, gossip and rumors, is destroying people and preventing them from growing into healthy and strong Christians.

As I look back I've realized that one of the great qualities of my father was that when you did something really bad and, you'd expect the worst from him, that was when he said nothing. He seemed to be able to sense the shame and guilt that you felt and, for him, there wasn't any need to add to it. He must have sensed that you had gotten the point. The lesson was self-evident, and it would be much more profitable for you to get on with life. I remember one time when I skipped school with some of my friends and we hitchhiked to Boston for the purpose of going to the Old Howard, which was a burlesque show. The odds would be probably one in a million that my father would ever see us entering, but he did. At the end of the show, we walked out to the street, and there he was. I nearly fell through the sidewalk. He said, "Oh, you had the day off? Do you want to go home with me?" He purchased tickets on the train for all of us, and carried on a normal conversation as though nothing had happened. When we got off the train, he offered my friends a ride home. As he left each of them off, I began to wonder what would happen to me when my last friend got out of the car, and the two of us would be alone. Nothing was said, and so then I felt it would be after supper or, worse still, he would tell Mom and I'd get it from both of them. He never raised it. It was in the past and forgotten! I can't recall him ever throwing up any of our past failings, especially the ones you felt ashamed of; for him, they were finished. Needless to say, he did deliver a message in his silence. He was an incredible man, and at his funeral I challenged the family by saying, "I hope that each of us can live out our values as well as Dad did." I'm still trying.

Thus, in the life of a wounded pilgrim each one is offered the opportunity and the challenge to accept, embrace our woundedness, whatever it might be, and to go on to grow into the fullness of the life of Christ. As I pointed out earlier, our woundedness is a given when we start the journey and we did not choose it—that is a fact! It is indeed a profound mystery, although the story of Adam and Eve is an attempt to explain it. Nevertheless, there remains the difficulty in understanding it, let alone in accepting it. It is an existential experience that no one escapes from. The Scriptures point out that even the just man, the holy man, falls seven times in the day and yet shall rise up again (Pr 24:10). Christ said, "If your brother does something wrong, rebuke him and, if he is sorry, forgive him" (Lk 17:3). And when Peter asked Christ how many times we should forgive our brother, Christ responded by saying, "Not seven, I tell you, but seventy-seven times" (Mt 18:22). Paul reminds us, "You were dead, because you were sinners and uncircumcised in body: he has brought you to life with him, he has forgiven us every one of our sins" (Col 2:13). "Receive the Holy Spirit. If you forgive anyone's sins, they are forgiven; if you retain anyone's sins, they are retained" (Jn 20:23). He even left us the sacrament of reconciliation.

In the life of dialogue, of friendship and love, there seems to be nothing quite as important as honesty. It has always been crucial, but it has become even more essential in our present time. In former times, for example, when someone entered marriage, the priesthood, or religious life, everyone took it for granted that it was forever. However, in our present climate, such a radical stand is no longer just taken for granted. Regardless of your own stand, the world looks on these commitments as being capable of negation. Today, you rarely hear about the responsibilities that flow from our own free choices and commitments, or for that matter, anything about the common good. There is an emphasis on the particular good, and that seems more and more to be determined by my feelings. It is, in my estimation, a sad state of things, and I fear for the future generations. There seem to be fewer and fewer people who are willing to pay the price for their free choices and hence the environmental factors so essential to society are being undermined: the family, the extended family, community, and the Church itself. I know from experience that my parents didn't always have a smooth ride, and perhaps they might well have wondered at times if it was all worth it. However, there were in place in those days values and principles which supported them in their commitment and enabled them to hang on and do the best they could. There was that deep sense of commitment that flowed from their free choice to enter marriage, and the same was true of the priesthood. I'm not saying that there aren't particular cases where a major choice involving commitment lacked the necessary freedom or that there couldn't be other circumstances that clearly indicate that the decision, the choice was wrong. Those things can and do happen, and it would be unjust and senseless to ask individuals in those situations to remain faithful to a commitment that has no real foundation. I merely want to stress the need for us to return to a proper sense of the common good for those who will follow us. There is always a need for models, and in this case for people who will pay the price, to the best of their ability, to live out their commitments.

The present cultural situation requires each of us to exercise prudence and to strive for honesty. I no longer, as a priest, can take for granted that by wearing the clerical collar, or whatever external sign there may be, that everyone else knows of my internal commitment. The same is also true of the married person—the ring on your finger no longer tells others that you are "not available." This came home to me in a powerful way when I was a graduate student at Catholic University. A provincial of an order of nuns asked me to celebrate Mass for their house of formation nearby, and to give some talks on the spiritual life. My first response was to explain that I was too busy, but she persisted and I finally agreed to do it, and I began to enjoy my weekly trips. It was my first experience of the awe that some people have in regard to Trappist monks, and the young nuns seemed surprised to find me human: he laughs! When I spoke they listened intently to every word that came out of me, since there had to be some kind of mystical content in words that came forth from a Trappist monk. There were a number of very attractive young women in the group, and I found myself enjoying their company, especially one in particular. We began to enjoy time together, and I became aware that I had strong feelings for her. It then became, for me, something like a Ping-Pong game, with the ball bouncing from one side of the net to the other. One side of me would say, "You have to deal with this in an honest way." The other side would say, "What are you going to do if you tell her you have these feelings and that you love her, and she thanks you but informs you she doesn't have the same feelings for you?" I sure didn't want to hear that! Then the little voice within me would say, "You're old enough to be her father!" But in response to that, on the other side of the net, I'd hear the response, "I'm losing my hair, but I'm still young and attractive." I finally went to see her in order to stop the Ping-Pong game, and to be honest. We took a walk and I told her how I felt, and she confided that she felt the same way for me. "Great!" I said. "Now we need to talk about this." "What do you want to talk about?" she replied. "Well, you're a sister and I, too, am a religious and also a priest—we need to talk about how to integrate all this into our commitments." She then said, "I wasn't thinking about that—I was thinking of the possibility of us getting married." I was shocked, and told her that I was committed to my vocation and that marriage was not a possibility. It worked out, but after some time, she left her community and did get married.

This experience brought home to me in a powerful way how essential it is to being honest in every relationship. Without an attempt to be honest, you can lead others into thinking that you are a free person, free from previous commitments and responsibilities. The anguish and hurt that flows from the games we play when honesty is not present is great, and the people in our lives are deeply affected. Love when coupled with touch, as I said earlier, requires a commitment to honesty. There is no escape from the obligation of raising questions in order to protect and support each dialogical relationship from becoming monological.

Each of us knows from our own lived experience that there are "slips between the cup and the lip." However, it is also true that the only thing that will ever prevent us ultimately from reaching our goal, perfect union with Christ, is that we choose to *quit!* St. Paul reminds us that "all things work out unto good, for those who love." That incredible moment when all things do come together and actually work out unto good is the work of the Holy Spirit, and He will never fail us! The mystics assure us that we need to be confident, that regardless of the temptations, faults, and failures we encounter, they can hinder us very little if we reach out to one another and to Christ for forgiveness. The author of *The Cloud of Unknowing* says, "The remnants of original sin (one of the givens) will plague you to the grave despite all your effort . . . but never give up and do not become overly anxious about failing."[7] For a long time on my own journey I used to say, "It's too good to be true!" Now, I can say with my whole being, "It's too good to be true, but it's *true!*"

One time I went to see the old abbot, Dom Edmund Futterer, and shared with him my discouragement in regards to not making much headway and in feeling terrible about all my past failures. After listening to my story he sent me off to look at a valuable tapestry that was located in the reception room of the monastery. He told me to observe the front and then to look at the back side of the tapestry, and then return. When I returned, he asked me what I had observed. I described the beauty of the front and especially the tone and colors in the background, and told him that the back side was chaotic with no beauty at all. He told me that life was something like a tapestry. The Holy Spirit was the artist and, for the most part, we rarely got a chance to see the beauty of the work of the artist— we saw only the back side. He said he would pray that one day I might get a peek at my tapestry and then I would see that if I eliminated from the work all that I didn't like about myself and all my faults and failures were wiped away, I would in fact destroy the beauty, the tone of the colors—the front would be as ugly as the back. Many years passed before I finally was given the opportunity of getting a peek at the front side, and I was amazed at what the artist had achieved. Recently, a person hearing this story gave me the following poem, which I share with you. I have no idea who the author is, perhaps it was the person who gave it to me.

TAPESTRY

My life is but a weaving
Between my God and me.
He chooses all the colors
And weaves on merrily.

Sometimes He chooses dark hues.
And I, in blinded pride,
Forget He sees the upper
And I the under side.

Not till the looms are silent
And the shuttles cease to fly
Shall God unroll the fabric
And show the unknown why.

The dark hues are as useful
In the weaver's skillful hand
As the strands of gold and silver
In the pattern He has planned.

In one of the last letters that Dom Edmund Futterer wrote he summed it all up when he said: "Now I'm beginning (note this word)—to realize that God has been in that poor, frustrated life all along; and it's a tremendous revelation of God's mercy. For long years I had seen the underside and the sight of my utter misery and frustration felt like a terrible weight bearing me down, while everything in my nature seemed to revolt and cry out: 'What's

the use—*cui bono?*' Now, thank God, I see something of
the upper side and my poor soul is amazed, for I see
clearly that the Spirit of God had been working all along,
drawing straight with crooked lines." As long as we never
quit, and continually seek to follow Christ, we will each
reach a similar point on our journey as Dom Edmund. We
will stand in awe of the beauty and power that God has
brought about and the fact that He does indeed draw
straight with crooked lines.

It is very important to know that intimacy and depth
relationships are *gifts*—they are the work of the Holy
Spirit in the unfolding process of a life of dialogue. One
must let the rhythm of the dialogue, the sharing flow on its
own course, in its own way, and in its own time toward
depth and intimacy. This hunger for intimacy has led
many to think that it is found only in bodily and sexual
intimacy, but, as I've already pointed out, this is an illusion
and leads not to true intimacy but to the loss of meaning
and even the possibility of intimacy. There are others who
have come to identify intimacy with the "spilling of one's
guts." There are even workshops today where participants can and do spill out their whole story. They stand
naked before one another and affirm each other, thinking
that is intimacy. It is not intimacy; it is nothing other than
pure manipulation and a violation of the whole process of
dialogue. Once at a convention, someone approached me
and went on to pour out the story of her life. I thanked her
for sharing with me, and assured her that God forgives
and that His love was unconditional. She then said, "I've
just shared with you all of the secrets of my life—aren't
you going to share yours?" I told her that I appreciated
the confidence she had placed in me in sharing her
secrets, but that I had no need or desire to share with her
my own. She then asked me if I wouldn't at least share one

aspect of my life, to which I told her that I wasn't going to share even a single "secret"! You tell me one secret, and I'll then tell you one; this is not dialogue, quite the contrary! It bespeaks a sick attitude and has nothing to do with intimacy. This type of revelation can be and almost always is manipulative and destructive to real intimacy.

One does need at least one person in one's life to whom a person could turn to and share anything that one wanted to reveal. In that person you know with certainty that he or she would remain steadfast, like the rock of Gibraltar, in communicating their unconditional love for you, just as you are! Each of us needs that person—a soul-friend! I continually remind people in my life that they never have to reveal anything to me as long as they can always close their eyes and hear me asking the question "Hey, do you know what?" and that they in their hearts know I love them just as they are. However, if they ever were to reach a point when they might doubt that my love was steadfast and that I could not accept them as they were, then, and then only, do they have to find me and reveal that which they think would cause me to reject them from my life. This is what true friendship, soul-friendship, is all about. Intimacy and soul-friendship are the products of the rhythm of dialogue, guided by the work of the Holy Spirit. Outside of a soul-friend, a spiritual friend, true intimacy doesn't exist and all our attempts to arrive at it will lead only to disillusionment and, at times, even disaster. This is especially true when one thinks that physical nakedness, and genital expression will bring it about. Quite the contrary, in fact. Although physical intimacy can be an expression of spiritual intimacy, it is more often than not mere manipulation—using another person as an object.

As we proceed on the journey it isn't long before we

discover that our ideals, values, and, yes, even our most solemn commitments are seldom perfectly realized in the concrete. As we've looked at the life of the wounded pilgrim, perhaps you have wondered, "But how do I move on?" "How do I deal, in a constructive way, with my woundedness?" I'm sure that, depending upon to whom you posed those questions, you'd get a variety of responses. Let me place before you only three approaches. They follow in sequence, with the third, in my estimation, being the most essential of the three.

The first is to open yourself to sharing with a true friend, a soul-friend. The Desert Fathers maintained that in merely surfacing our thoughts and problems that take away our inner peace, we receive the light we need and regain that inner peace. The Holy Spirit dwells within us, our Spiritual Director, and when we seek to deal with life situations, He helps us to face them in a positive and constructive way. Sharing with a true friend can create the necessary environment that provides us with insights, understandings, and the courage to face things.

The second approach is to seek professional help, someone who has the expertise to help us sort out the situation in a way that we can constructively deal with it. Such a person could be a competent spiritual director, a psychologist, or a psychiatrist. Father Dominic Maruca, S.J., sets before us in a very clear and precise way the aims and methods of these professional people under the heading of:

CARING RELATIONSHIPS

	AIM	METHOD
Guidance (Education)	To increase understanding and thereby enable a person to be	Imparting knowledge or advice that is accurate and appropriate,

CARING RELATIONSHIPS

	AIM	METHOD
	an intelligent and responsible agent in making an immediate decision.	historical and contemporary.
Counseling (Psychology)	To help a person increase his/her ability to relate in ways that satisfy his/her basic personality needs. To facilitate growth and minor adjustment through enhanced self-awareness and constructive changes in behavior.	Creating an empathetic relationship that assists to gain insight and objective clarification. Helping a client to see that living in self-contradictory ways violate one's sense of justice, integrity and respect for persons is a cause and not just a symptom of inner conflicts.
Psychotherapy (Psychiatry)	To heal a person who is suffering from incapacitating distress due to unmet needs and deep conflicts	Through the corrective emotional experience, called transference, the patient experiences and expresses what he/she formerly experienced in reference to significant persons in his/her past life. The patient unconsciously transfers or projects onto the therapist; then these trans-

CARING RELATIONSHIPS

AIM	METHOD
	ferred wishes and feelings are analyzed and worked through.
Spiritual Direction Gracefully to assist a fellow Christian in gaining a clearer understanding of commitment.	Through a dialogical process of action and reflection, two pilgrims discuss God's invitation to more intimate communion with Him, through an ongoing companionship with His Son and Spirit in effecting growth.

There are times on the journey that each of us can benefit from seeking help from professional resource persons such as are described above. It is indeed necessary at some points on our pilgrimage to do this in order to break from the bonds that cripple us from being fully the Child of God, and to regain our inner freedom and peace.

The third and most necessary element in our daily lives is prayer—spending time with God each day of our journey. St. Teresa of Ávila points out that no matter how far you go in the life of prayer and union with God, you can still fall and that it is essential that you never *QUIT* spending time with God, day in and day out. All of the mystics and spiritual authors confirm this—without a regular prayer life you run a very dangerous course. Prayer allows us to step back from our daily preoccupations and allows us to hear the Word of God in all kinds of ways. Prayer gives you the opportunity to look at your life under the light of the Scriptures. It allows God to heal you, to give you strength, and to renew the power of the Holy Spirit in your daily life. It is essential!

Prayer opens a way of handling our faults, failures, and even sins in a constructive way. In the earlier days of my journey I would tend to pray only when I felt worthy of meeting Him. I thought that I was unworthy to put myself in His Presence when I didn't have things put together, and so my prayer life was a series of beginnings. It was in the monastery that I found a new understanding of prayer, and discovered I couldn't strive to follow Him without it. There have been times when I felt tempted to give up that time with Him for some other particular activity, but I know from experience that I must spend time with Him each day. I'm not about to say how much time one should spend in prayer, but some time each day is critical, necessary—it is very important!

As you develop your prayer life you'll discover, if you already are not aware of it, that it is all about a relationship —a friendship with God. As with friends whom you see, hear, and share with, so prayer brings you to a growing awareness of the Presence of the Friend who dwells within you. You'll find yourself reaching out to Him in all kinds of situations. You'll confide in Him and talk with Him, as one with Whom you can share anything. You'll likewise learn to listen to Him. It is an experience that is most difficult to describe, but perhaps if you'd take a moment and reflect on a particular friendship that has enriched your life and allowed you to share deeply, then multiply that by an infinite number and you'll arrive at some idea as to the relationship and intimacy that He offers each of us.

You need to come to a point where you deal with God as

a friend: one to whom you can turn to and just "be." He is always present to us, hears us, and responds to us in so many different ways. As the author of *The Cloud of Unknowing* pointed out, the only other one that He needs is you! Without you, there can be no relationship, no friendship.

As you develop this relationship of friendship with Him, you'll discover an ability to, as they say, let your hair down. When you feel lonely, yell out to Him and ask Him where He is and that you need Him. When you fall down, run to Him and talk to Him. "Hey, friend, where were you? You knew I was going to make a mess out of that situation, and look what's happened! Next time, get here earlier!" In running to Him in every situation, you'll discover that He will always embrace you, forgive you, and just like beautiful snow falling on all of the ugliness of the mess we make of our environment and covering it in a blanket of beauty, so too will He cover everything with the beauty of His unconditional love.

When I was a young child we were taught that if there had never been original sin we would have lived without wars, and all of the burdens that we now carry—the world would have been a just and loving place to live in. They had a song in those days which was sung a great deal, especially in Lent, "O Felix Culpa" (O Beautiful Fault). One day I was with my mom at the Lenten devotions in the afternoon after school, and they started to sing that song. I leaned over to Mom and whispered, "Mom, why do they say that original sin was a beautiful fault?" My mother replied, "Because through that fault Christ came!" "But, Mom, the nuns say that if we didn't have original sin we'd all be happy and there wouldn't be any of the problems we now have." She replied to me, saying, "But we would never have known Christ!" With that I said, "I think that we would have been better off if He had stayed in Heaven, and we were all happy!" With that I received a loving rap on the head; with a stern look, she said, "Don't ever say that again!"

We need to gather up all of our sins and faults and each of us should sit down and write our own song, "O Beautiful Faults!" Through sin, failures, and faults come compassion, mercy, forgiveness, and the experience of unconditional love, which in actual fact transcends all of our sins and faults. Your faults are the occasion to reach out to your neighbor, to God, and through that reaching out you can receive forgiveness. There is nothing quite so disarming as when someone reaches out to you, and you have the power, the Gift, to listen, to be for them, accept them, and even to forgive! You are always enriched through such an encounter, and it is, to say the least, a very humbling experience. Remember, forgiveness is one of the Gifts of the Holy Spirit.

Our failures always raise our consciousness of the need for God and for one another. Our inherent weaknesses are the very foundations from which we have power, as St. Paul tell us. God is not about to give His power to anyone until He is absolutely sure that you'll never take credit for His gifts. This utter dependence upon Him is a direct result of being in touch with our woundedness and being in touch is related to the experience of failure. St. Teresa of Ávila insists that the first thing we must do in wanting to become whole, to be healed, is to accept and embrace ourselves as we are. Only when we have taken ownership of ourselves can God begin the process of healing us and bringing us to wholeness. He will infallibly accomplish this, in His time and way—not ours! The only thing that can prevent this total transformation is if we quit!

Let go of the past, let go of your sins—they have been forgiven and He has embraced you, as you are. He has laid down His life for you—His love is unconditional! Spend time with Him in prayer. Prayer is what brings about the internalization of the Good News, and frees us to be the children of God. Prayer is the source of integration; it is where the Holy Spirit teaches you how to follow Christ. In prayer you'll come to taste and know Him and you'll discover that He does have you in the palm of His hand. He knows you by name, and He loves you without any conditions—not waiting for you to become perfect. He loves you as you are! "Too good to be true . . . but *true!*"

"THE WINDS OF GOD'S GRACE ARE ALWAYS BLOWING, BUT WE MUST MAKE AN EFFORT TO RAISE OUR SAILS."

REFLECTIONS

1. Describe the qualities that you've found present in dialogical and monological relationships. What have you learned from these relationships?

2. What does love mean to you? What does it involve? Identify some relationships in which you have experienced love.

3. Reflect upon the integration of your emotions, passions, and sexual feelings in a given relationship. Can you identify the times when you didn't have the integration? What did you learn from these situations?

SUGGESTED READINGS

1. Henri J. M. Nouwen. *The Wounded Healer.* Doubleday, 1972.

2. Thomas J. Tyrell. *Urgent Longings: Reflections on the Experience of Infatuation, Human Intimacy, and Contemplative Love.* Affirmation Books, 1980.

3. Victor E. Frankl. *Man's Search for Meaning.* Washington Square Press, 1963.

4. Joseph Goldbrunner. *Holiness Is Wholeness.* University of Notre Dame Press, 1964.

CHAPTER VI

THE LIFE OF PRAYER AND DISCIPLINE

The preceding chapters have been so many building blocks which form the underpinnings that can support the most important single ingredient essential to your journey, which is *prayer!* Although it is the most important aspect of your pilgrimage, it is also one that causes a great deal of difficulty for many. I have come to believe that this is mainly due to the view we have of what a life of prayer is. On the other side of the coin, there is discipline, and these two go hand in hand. You would find it a profitable exercise if you would take a few moments and identify some of the significant people in your life who helped to shape your view of prayer and discipline. What did they teach you?

I, myself, went back in my own journey to locate the beginning point of my understanding and grasp of what prayer and discipline were, and then walked along my journey looking at various times when my horizon-view opened up and the impact that had on me. In my early formation the two significant people who shaped my views were my mother and father.

My father was very traditional in his approach to

prayer, and for him prayer was, like for most people of his generation, doing something—you said your prayers! He had dozens of little novena booklets, and various devotions which sustained him and helped him on his journey. When you prayed, his viewpoint was that you had to kneel, and kneel straight up! When we prayed the rosary, we all had to kneel, but my mother always sat in the most comfortable chair in the living room. Inevitably one of us would interrupt the prayer and ask if we could sit with Mom, because our kneecaps were hurting from the kneeling. His response would always be *"No!* You're praying and you should be kneeling!" "But, Dad, how come Mom can sit down and pray?" He would then turn to her and say, "You see, you're giving scandal to the kids! You should be on your knees when you pray!" As always, she would calmly look at him and say, "You pray the way you want, and I'll pray my way!"

If you spoke to my father about a problem you were having, he would almost always go and fetch one of his novena booklets and tell you to read it for the next seven days. If Mom overheard him saying that to you, then when you passed through the kitchen to go out, she would whisper to you, "Don't bother with his booklets, just go and spend some time quietly with God!" In those days the custom was that you went to confession every Saturday night, and my father checked to be sure that you went, either in the afternoon or the evening. As I said earlier, on one occasion we came out of the Church after confession and my father asked my mother if she had confessed that she had not gone to Mass on the preceding Sunday. She reminded him that some of the kids were sick and that, if there was any fault involved then, it was God's fault that the kids got sick and that she missed Mass. My father thought that she should go back to the priest and test it out, but my mother told him that she had no problem in missing Mass to take care of a child, and that if he had a problem, then he should go see the priest. It was a tense ride home that evening.

My father instilled within each of us the need to pray, and he showed us a variety of ways of praying through the novenas and devotions of that day. The Mass was central to his life, and there was hardly a day that went by without him going to Mass, which at times required great sacrifice. His rosary and visits to the Blessed Sacrament were also very important to him. Above all, he had a simple faith in God's Providence, and would often say to us, "It's providential—it's God's plan!" Nevertheless, prayer for him involved doing something, mostly "saying your prayers." That was his "viewpoint" and he lived it out on his journey.

My mother approached prayer from a different point of view. For her, prayer was very special, unique to each person, and that it had far less to do with doing something, or saying your prayers. The emphasis, for her, was in just "being" with God, not doing something or saying some words, but in spending quiet time with Him. She took me one day to the sea wall and as we sat there looking out on to the ocean, she explained to me how important and necessary it was for me to learn how to listen to God in my life and spend time with Him. She said that I had to learn to listen to Him in the sea, in the wind, in the events and people who would enter my life. She also explained to me how important it was to have some spots where I could go and just be with Him. She concluded her little instruction, and they were rare events, by telling me that Christ was my closest friend and would always be with me—He was inside of me and that I should be His good friend.

They both had their own approaches to prayer and

their fidelity to their views brought them very close to God, and at the end of their journeys they both radiated an inner peace and tranquillity—everything came together and they were ready to meet their God. The difficulty for me personally was that from the time that Mom gave me her little "conference" on prayer, I never encountered any support for her approach until I entered the monastery. Your viewpoint of prayer is critical because from it flows the very expression of prayer, whether it be saying prayers or doing something—or just resting in His presence.

Prayer has been traditionally described in various ways, but basically it is rooted in terms of relationship—God and the individual, and the community. It has been described as an opening of the heart, an encounter, contact, awareness, or experience of Him. In each instance we find ourselves in the category of relationship with God revealing Himself, extending an invitation, and leaving us free to respond or not to. This revelation may take place in solitude, community, reading, encounters with others, and countless other ways. Our loving response to God's Presence in any of these situations is, prayer. Karl Rahner says that "the Commandment of Love is more than the fulfillment of the Law: it is also the essence of all true prayer."[1]

There have been individuals in the past, and there are some in our midst today, who would like to restrict prayer to certain very specific occasions or moments. It seems impossible to understand this position in the light of the Scriptures. The New Testament tells us that we ought "to pray continually and never lose heart" (Lk 18:1). St. Paul speaks very strongly in terms of prayer embracing our whole life when he says, "keep praying in the Spirit on every possible occasion" (Ep 6:18), "pray constantly" (1 Th 5:18), and furthermore, to "keep praying regularly"

(Rm 12:12). The early monks endeavored to live these injunctions through memorizing the Scriptures, and attempted to pray unceasingly through the practice of repeating short phrases of the Scriptures as they wove and unwove baskets. The history of the "Jesus Prayer" in Eastern spirituality points to the same desire to pray always. Various religious founders, and foundresses, attempted to construct a series of "spiritual exercises" which would hopefully tend to help the individual to go forth in a spirit of meeting and responding to God, from moment to moment.

Seemingly, there is a contradiction for the Christian of our time who embraces the injunction to pray, but who also has all kinds of concerns and obligations particular to his/her state in life: mother, father, doctor, lawyer, laborer, stockbroker, or whatever. Can the Christian compartmentalize his/her life, or must one attempt to integrate it? Can we restrict prayer to one special area of a person's life?

As we looked at the dialogical life, it became quite obvious that you can't live it without a commitment to prayer in opting for a life of love. In choosing to follow Christ, each of us has chosen to develop and perfect the art of "spiritual communication." "God is love, and whoever remains in love remains in God and God in him" (1 Jn 4:16). Rahner maintains that the love of God and love of neighbor are ontologically the same. In loving my neighbor, in and by that act, I am also loving God!

The life of dialogue requires one to meet each unfolding moment of reality in a spirit of openness, being total, disciplined, and related. One cannot approach "moments" in this way without "love"! If we accept that prayer is union with God, an encounter with Him, then we must, it seems to me, conclude that the dialogical person is praying as he/she meets moments in a loving way. One's moments bring various types of realities—moments of solitude, work, recreation, encounters with others, study, reading. In every situation one must attempt to meet the reality and responsibilities of the moment authentically in dialogue if one is to meet God.

As the life of dialogue deepens, so the life of prayer also deepens. It is impossible to comprehend the depth of relationship we have with the Person (God) whom we have never seen, without first comprehending the depth we have with those whom we do see! We know that in those relationships that have become true friendships, we have had to undergo purifications, trials, and various kinds of difficulties as the unfolding process of address and response took place. Soul-friends do arrive at a point in their relationship where they can communicate their commitment and love by way of signs and symbols. Such relationships, as Aelred pointed out, transcend themselves, and we are infallibly led into the presence of the person whom we have not seen, but who by faith we know dwells within each of us. St. Irenaeus once said that when two people love each other, it is God loving God! The Scriptures relate to us over and over again that the yardstick for judging our love for God is our love for one another. "Anyone who says 'I love God' and hates his brother, is a liar, since whoever does not love the brother whom he can see cannot love God whom he has not seen" (1 Jn 4:20).

It is indeed impossible for the dialogical person to avoid the invitation, or refuse the response to a personal dialogue with God. The response, in the past, has been identified, described, and named. You will, at times, find yourself reaching out to God and asking Him to help you deal with certain situations in the context of His love. This was named "the prayer of petition." Your heart will, at times, burst forth in thanksgiving. This was named "the prayer of thanksgiving." You will find yourself continually returning to the Scriptures, reflecting and pondering His message. This was named *lectio divina*—"spiritual reading." *Lectio divina,* traditionally was viewed as a dialogue, an interchange of knowledge and love with God, and the Scriptures were the primary font of that interchange. During the course of time this font of knowledge and love was extended beyond the Scriptures. Our recent heritage embraced the above and described and named other forms of prayer. However, many individuals embraced a particular form and failed to grasp the unity of the Life of Prayer.

St. Vincent de Paul once said to the Daughters of Charity that if they were called from the chapel to answer the door, they should not think that they were leaving Christ, but merely were meeting Him in a new way. "The Sacrament of the Moment," popularized by the Jesuit de Causade, stresses that each moment is a sacrament in which God is revealing Himself, most often in a hidden way, but nevertheless present! It takes great discipline to live in the "real world," where God is, and not to create our own little world where it becomes impossible to find God. Hence, we must be prepared to meet, to respond to, to encounter God in each changing moment—this is what true prayer is all about.

Today, it is most difficult not to embrace the view that each person is unique, and that every relationship is unique—never to be duplicated! Thus, it becomes evident that we can only articulate the principles that each individual faces: the task of internalizing them and giving a unique expression to them in and through their unique, never to be duplicated, journey. Indeed, it is impossible, if not crazy, to legislate methods of how one is to grow in the "art of spiritual communication." Rahner puts it profoundly when he speaks of the impossibility "of giving a theoretical definition not only to the 'law of life' of the individual Christian, but also to the 'gift' granted by the Spirit to the individual ages of the world and to the Church . . . it is ultimately impossible to deduce from laws." Thus, each of us must come to grips with one's own relationship with God, which is called prayer!

At the very heart of the Christian message stands the bold assertion "God is Love!" The person of faith begins with John's pregnant affirmation, "God is Love," and allows it to lead him/her where the Spirit wills. While being led by the Spirit we begin to accept that we are made in the image and likeness of "Love." Love, then, is the Alpha and the Omega of our very existence. Our Lord spoke of only one commandment as specifically His: "This is my commandment: love one another, as I have loved you" (Jn 15:12). We have already seen that the love of God and the love of one's friend grow simultaneously. When one is authentically intensified, so too is the other. Everything and everyone is an occasion for meeting God—the Christian is challenged to see life in terms of integration, not in the separation of compartments. True discipline is not withdrawal, but a radical openness to and an active acceptance of the person, the task, or the event that the moment brings. Thus, the Christian seizes the moment as the expression of the continuing Incarnational life of Christ. Martin Buber spoke of the importance of living in the moment when he said: "I know no fullness but each mortal hour's fullness of claim and responsibility. Though far from being equal to it, yet I know that in the claim I am claimed and may respond in responsibility, and know who speaks and demands response. I do not know much more.

If that is religion, then it is just everything, simply all that is lived in its possibility of dialogue."[2]

Hans Urs von Balthasar speaks of prayer as being something "more than an exterior act performed out of a sense of duty, an act in which we tell God various things he already knows, a kind of daily attendance in the presence of the Sovereign who awaits, morning and evening the submission of his subjects. . . . prayer is an exchange between God and the soul, and because, in this exchange, a definite language is used, obviously that of God Himself. It can be looked upon as conversation. Prayer is a dialogue, not a monologue recited by men in God's presence."[3]

Since all knowledge and love of God is based on analogy, it becomes key to embrace the knowledge and experience of love in those "visible" relationships that we have, in order to know something of the "invisible" relationship we have with God. Just as the life of love and friendship is an ongoing process of growth and development, so too is our friendship with God. It requires a constant effort and a perseverance that can come only from a deep personal commitment. Otherwise, one will drift from a life of love into a life of selfishness. Prayer, then, as my good friend and colleague Father Ernie Larkin, O. Carm., so often says, "is in life and comes out of life. Life is its matrix and proving ground."

From my early childhood until I entered the monastery, I struggled to grasp the meaning and to understand the life of prayer. There were times when prayer gave me consolation and a deep inner peace, which made it easy for me to return for other periods of prayer. However, there was a great deal of in-between times when I did very little, if any, praying. Deep down I felt the need and wanted it to make sense to me, and above all I wanted prayer to become a part of me and not the result of "shoulds" and "oughts." When I was a young monk, my eyes were opened by the Holy Spirit, who showed me what had been all along present in my heritage but which I had never seen before. The statement that was the source of this new light for me was from one of the early Church Fathers and it opened up a whole new world of understanding for me, "A training in prayer is a training in friendship."

The Center for Human Development's work with priests, religious, and laity has shown that there are two major problems: one is the loss of trust and the other is the lack of consistency in the life of prayer—spending time with God day in and day out, regardless of what might happen. The problem in prayer is rooted, in my belief, in what I often refer to as a "vacuum" in regards to our rich heritage—the teachings of the Church Fathers and our mystical tradition. It has been neglected for far too long and needs to be surfaced for the people of our own time. Often, individuals quit praying, being consistent in spending time with God each day, because they have gone beyond their present form of prayer and when they continue to try to force that form to provide inner meaning and relevance, they find themselves up against a wall— there is no meaning, and the form or way they had prayed until now is no longer the proper vehicle in expressing their ongoing relationship to God. But without knowledge of how to continue in a way in this relationship, they can misinterpret their sense of loss and remove themselves from spending time with God, in favor of at least making constructive use of their time by getting more involved in other areas of their lives.

If you've been operating out of a framework of prayer that is anything other or less than the framework of friendship, then you will, if you haven't already, experience the difficulty of remaining faithful to time with the Lord, day in and day out, and no doubt will quit! You will return to praying off and on due to feelings of guilt or through "shoulds" and "oughts." The framework of friendship will help you, but even here one must realize that without discipline, perseverance, and faith one will fall by the wayside.

The following diagram puts before you a way of looking at the development of true friendship and the name that we have traditionally given to each succeeding stage of growth in intimacy with The Friend Who dwells within us.

STAGES OF RELATIONSHIP— DEVELOPMENT OF FRIENDSHIP

STEPS	AIM	METHOD	PRAYER
Beginning	to develop a friendship	conversations concerning mutual interests	Vocal
Progressing	to know one another	an honest sharing of feelings and inner life	Meditation and Affective
Attainment	intimacy	spending time with one another, enjoying the beauty and love you've found	Contemplation

In the past there tended to be an emphasis on vocal prayer, with few being encouraged to enter meditative and affective prayer, let alone contemplative prayer. In my estimation, this was due to the lack of understanding of our rich heritage. Even for those who entered the priesthood and religious life, contemplative prayer was not seen as a normal development in their prayer lives. Contemplative prayer was only for those who had been able to conquer all their faults, and were "giants" in the life of virtue. Indeed, if you aspired to contemplative prayer, you needed to leave this terrible world we live in and join a contemplative order. Only within the cloistered walls could one hope to receive this gift of contemplative prayer. The above viewpoints are, needless to say, pure heresies—every Christian is called to union with God, to intimacy and friendship with Him. That's exactly why we are created, why He sent His son, and why Christ died for us. The old manuals on the spiritual life stress that contemplative prayer is a gift, but then went on to identify all the necessary dispositions we needed in order to receive the gift. It's like as if God were there dangling a carrot before us and saying if we become perfect He might give it to us. Crazy as all this might seem, it nevertheless was the framework that many of us grew up with. However, the mystics and saints describe it quite differently and continually remind us of how God longs to bring us to union with Him. This union with Him is indeed a gift which He can bestow anytime He desires, but it is usually received in and through the struggle of following Him.

What happens in those relationships which you can see, feel, and experience and which invite you to intimacy but go no further than the point of knowing one another? They fail to enter that incredible space where you can communicate a thousand different ways: through a smile or a wink, or just by sitting in silence communicating through mutual presence. Do you look forward to seeing people who have invited you to the land of intimacy but for one reason or another have stopped the process of growth into intimacy? Isn't it true that such relationships that were exciting, rewarding, and which you looked forward to each encounter lose all of that and dry up when they freeze on a given plateau? And isn't it also true that you finally become bored and eventually quit putting forth the energies that once seemed to cost so little— because there just isn't any place for that relationship to go?

Vocal prayer is the starting point. From there we do want to come to know the Lord. That desire brings us to meditation, and this was always described as the method of "getting to know the Lord." Getting to know Him was achieved by meditating on the Scriptures, which is a primary source of His self-revelation. Once you begin to know Him and you force yourself to continue this method, refusing to open yourself to go beyond this stage, for whatever reasons, then your meditations which once were so powerful in motivating you and inspiring you will begin to dry up. Once they dry up, you too become bored and tired, and have to drag yourself to the encounter which no longer, seemingly, has any meaning—you'll quit!

St. Teresa of Ávila, in describing the prayer life, uses the image of watering a garden. There is a well near the garden and you go there to fetch the water. You lower the bucket down the well and, when it is full, you haul it up and then carry it to the garden. This is, obviously, hard work, but it's worth it since you're able to see the flowers begin to blossom and finally break forth in all their beauty —this is exactly what happens in the early stage of prayer. The work is very rewarding and you feel that you've done something—the emphasis is on you! She points out that there is another way of watering the garden; while still involving some work, nevertheless it is much easier and more productive. That is when we install a water wheel and an aqueduct which will carry the water to the garden. True, we still have to turn the wheel, but it is far less demanding than fetching the water with the bucket. You're still doing some work, and here is where the soul endeavors to be recollected in His presence. She goes on to explain that we can move the garden near the river or stream, and the water will then just seep through the soil and take care of the garden. The Holy Spirit has begun to take over our prayer life, and now it is time to set aside our own little "work" and let Him lead us. This is contemplative prayer. Finally, Teresa explains that the garden can best be watered by the rain—union with God!

Thus, when we start out on the life of prayer we don't mind the work, in fact we enjoy it. You have the great feeling that you did something. Of course, there is a great deal of self-satisfaction and some pride in this effort of ours. Hence, God will infallibly allow the water to dry up in the well, and then it becomes quite difficult to continue to go to the well when we know there isn't any water there. We also feel torn and full of grief over watching the flowers we watered wilt and die. What He is trying to do in and through all of this is to get us to let go of all our little activities and ways of relating to Him and just rendezvous and be with Him, allowing the Holy Spirit to pray within you. This is very difficult, since we have lost the feeling of having done something. When you're with a soul-friend enjoying the intimacy, that incredible gift which is so enriching, do you feel you are doing nothing? Perhaps others watching you, just sitting there, being together, might ask, "What did you do?" When you'd respond "Oh! We were just together," they might think you were crazy to be wasting such valuable time—at least you could have been discussing world events, or the rise and fall of the stock market!

Some of the flowers that I found in the garden of my own journey were very special for me and sources of great help in praying and trying to love God. However, each time the flower would eventually dry up, in spite of all my effort to continue to water it and care for it—so that I could once again find the inspirations and insights that the flower once gave. Each time it was as if He would say, "Vincent, come with Me. I want to show you the rest of the garden and all the other flowers," and I would say, "Thanks for the invitation, but I like my 'rose' and I'm not interested in the other flowers." He thus had no alternative, in my case, but to let the rose wilt and die before He could get me to even look at the other flowers. It took me a long time to learn the lesson to let go, and so my precious flowers would wilt and die—it was a very painful experience. My "roses" over the years were the Scriptures, favorite spiritual authors, devotions, and other ways that He spoke to me, and through which I felt uplifted and close to Him. Today, at best, I can only go back to those roses and give thanks for the day when they radiated beauty and were incredible sources of light and inspiration for me. Each one of them were sources of wonder and feelings of great love for the Lord.

It took me some time to grasp and understand that the intimacy that He was calling me to had little, if anything, to do with me or my strengths and virtues, but it had everything to do with Him and His unconditional love for me. He slowly taught me that He is the source of my strength, my Comforter, and that His love, mercy and compassion are all steadfast. He is always there, and I need only to put my total trust in Him and spend time with Him. My failures only make me more aware of my need for Him, and thus always bring me immediately back to Him. We are reminded in the Scriptures that He is a jealous God and is not about to give us His power until He has you in the palm of His hand and you'll never take credit for His work, which He accomplishes in and through you. As the author of *The Cloud of Unknowing* points out, it is essential to be grounded in humility, both imperfect and perfect. Thus, the faults and failures that flow from our human frailty, our "given" weaknesses, are meant to bring us ever deeper and deeper into humility and become departure points into a greater intimacy with Him.

St. Teresa of Ávila points out over and over again, in her works, that the worst thing you can do is to quit praying— spending time with the Lord each day. She tells us that even in advanced stages of prayer, one can still fall, which she admits happened to her. We each carry different burdens, different crosses. We are indeed wounded people. St. Paul tried desperately to get the Lord to remove from him a given weakness. In refusing to do this, Jesus allowed Paul to discover that his power was not in his strength, but in his weakness. It was one of the few times that Paul remained silent, so we can each think that perhaps the thing that Paul struggled with is what we also struggle with. Hopefully, we too will discover that our weaknesses are the source of our strength and power because of Christ. The mystics and saints are *not* telling us to sin, but they are telling us that we should turn to Christ in our weakness and above all remain faithful to prayer, wasting time with the Master; He will infallibly heal us in His way and in His time. He desires that we reach the full union with Him and to discover integration and wholeness. Only an infidelity to prayer will prevent that from taking place. We must never quit praying, spending time with Him each day!

"Wasting time with the Master" was a popular saying in the early days, and needs to be rediscovered in our own time with its emphasis on efficiency, time competency, and productivity, which can undermine the value of just, "wasting time" with Him and with those who are close to us. We can become too busy and lose a sense of deeper values. We have relegated to children the luxury of play and wasting time, and as each of us enters adulthood, it becomes nearly impossible to hold on to these. It has been said that, the person who has lost the ability to play has also lost the ability to pray. Leisure is also a necessary disposition which fosters the growth in both wisdom and friendship, and yet we have left this for retirement! Our cultural phenomenon has put us on the merry-go-round, and we have lost some of the key elements to living life well. Their absence makes the call to intimacy in prayer and in friendship all the more difficult to achieve. There are some, as a result, who have arrived at a point where they believe that good works, and a few short prayers on the run, is all that is needed. Our tradition, though, insists that a regular time in our daily life for wasting time with the Master is an absolute necessity. Without it, you'll find it most difficult to meet each moment with that inner peace and beauty that invites others to dialogue and allows you to experience the Lord in a thousand different ways.

One of the difficulties is that when all the changes came after Vatican II, there were priests, religious, and lay who challenged, ridiculed, and laughed at many of the devotions and ways of praying. They dispensed with them and, in my estimation, failed to replace them, leaving people in a vacuum. People who hungered for an inner, spiritual life often found themselves lost and without direction. In general, it can be said that priests were trained for sacramental ministry and not for the role of spiritual leader and guide. Hence, they were ill equipped by their training to fill this vacuum. It is even more difficult to understand how, in this day, many seminary programs still lack the necessary formation in spirituality for young candidates to the priesthood. For me, it is shocking, when speaking to deacons concerning their training in Ascetical and Mystical Theology, to discover they only had one course, or none at all. Most of them acknowledge that they have had no formal training in our rich mystical heritage. Patrology and Spiritual Theology have seemingly been relegated to the unimportant. Priests are rarely sent on for graduate work in the field of spirituality. Other fields are also important, but at the same time, the work of the Center for Human Development confirms the crying need for competently trained people to minister to the spiritual needs of the people of God! Ministers in other denominations embraced the behavioral sciences as a way of ministering to people. However, in the Center's work with the Ministry to Ministers Program, and the Ministry to Chaplains Program with the U.S. Armed Forces, we have discovered that they hunger to discover our heritage in spirituality. It was to this common heritage of spirituality that Paul VI, interestingly, pointed as the starting point for true ecumenical dialogue, which could establish a fundamental understanding, leading to possible unity.

The vacuum opened the doors for those from the East, bearing all kinds of goodies, which people flocked to discover. Transcendental Meditation became the "in thing"! People who devoted two twenty-minute periods each day to this method were assured of lower blood pressure, inner tranquillity, and a release of their potential. Laypeople, along with priests and religious, participated in these training programs as a way of filling the void. During that time I happened to be giving a speech in a diocese, and afterward a priest approached me just as I was having a chat with the bishop, who had the reputation of being an old conservative. The priest asked me what I thought of TM and the bishop started to walk away, but the priest asked him if he would return to listen to my response. I felt like I was being set up, and I asked the priest why he wanted to know. He then went on to tell the bishop and myself that the TM people had offered to come to his parish and give the TM training program to all the parishioners at a reduced price. In those days people were paying around $150 per person, and they had offered him the bargain rate of only $100 for each couple in the parish. I asked him how many couples he had in his parish, and he said there were approximately a thousand. I said, "Gosh! that's a lot of money!" I then turned to the bishop and said, "Bishop, would you release Father for a few days and we'll teach him the method of using 'holy words' and what our tradition offers in the area of Centering Prayer, and then when he returns we'll undercut the TM offer. He can then teach this old method in other parishes for $50 a couple. Twenty-five dollars will stay in the parish and the other $25 will go to the diocese." The bishop quickly replied, "Father, when can you go?" And with that, the priest walked away.

TM can certainly help people, and does foster recollection. However, it lacks the depth of our rich heritage and fails to foster the life of friendship with the Lord who dwells within us. Our own heritage in regards to our prayer life is rich in methods that assist us in recollection, being quiet, and drawing close to Christ in friendship, which in turn gives us that deep inner peace and tranquillity. In experiencing His peace, you will find an ability to face the ups and downs of life. Prayer will help you to move away from the enslavement of anxieties and establish you in tranquillity. The primary concern that flows from our heritage is not to lower your blood pressure or anything other than to foster the growth in intimacy with the Lord. A fidelity to prayer in our tradition will certainly promote your physical and psychological well being, but that flows from your union with God! There is in our tradition what has been called the "Prayer of Quiet," the "Prayer of Faith," which today are being referred to as "Centering Prayer." TM responded to a vacuum, and from that experience many have been surprised to discover that all along, within our own tradition, there existed a method which could respond to their needs.

To pray, using this method, one must first take a comfortable position, which varies from person to person. You might at one point find kneeling or sitting comfortable. At another time you might find yourself in a hospital bed and unable to take a comfortable position, and yet still able to use the method. To start, I'd recommend you try sitting on an upright chair, with your feet on the floor. You then identify a holy word or short phrase which you will use to foster your recollection and quiet time with the Lord. It will serve as a tool to bring you back to resting in His Presence when distractions come, and they will come! Perhaps you have a favorite passage in Scripture, the shorter the better, as the author of *The Cloud of Unknowing* tells us. Words and phrases such as God, Jesus, Help me, Have mercy on me, or some similar types can be used. It is also very helpful if you can find a quiet place at home, in a Church, or some other place that offers you silence and quiet. Having taken your seat on the chair, close your eyes and place yourself in His presence, the Friend who

dwells within you. Now, just be quiet in His Presence—
say nothing and do nothing. If you find yourself distracted
by thoughts, just return to the word or the phrase you've
chosen, and go back to being quiet, wasting time with
Him. You will no doubt find it difficult to be quiet at first,
but slowly the Holy Spirit will teach you and you'll look
forward to this "quiet" time with your Friend. You'll also
discover that during the day you'll feel drawn at times to
the source of your inner peace, to the Friend who dwells
within you. You'll have a new strength that will allow you
to deal with others and daily events in a way that promotes the growth of all.

There are many today, some being my colleagues, who
would stress that you need to do this for twenty to thirty
minutes twice a day, or at least once a day. I have discovered that many people get discouraged when they can't
persevere day in, and day out—things come up, pressing
needs, and time passes quickly. They then find that the
twenty or thirty minutes is too difficult or unattainable
each and every day, so, they quit! Let me place before you
an alternative to quitting. If I could get you to just take
three minutes twice a day, as a minimum of time with the
Lord. Sometimes the three minutes might well expand to
much more, but I stress *never less* than three minutes
twice a day. I guarantee you that you will make great
progress in the life of prayer, and furthermore, it will
become impossible for you ever to drift away from the
Lord.

It becomes impossible for you to abandon God in your
life when you consistently, day in and day out, rendezvous
with Him twice a day, putting yourself in His Presence
and just being with Him. You cannot do this and at the
same time be at odds with Him. You cannot pray in the
above manner if you have fallen and failed to turn to Him,

saying, "I'm sorry!" Once you have turned to Him for forgiveness, you can then, and then only, enter within and "waste time" with Him. Fidelity to daily time in prayer is an absolute necessity and certainly each of us can find three minutes twice a day. Again, I point out that if you spend more, even a half hour, that's fine, but, never less than the three minutes. If you can't even find three minutes twice a day that you could make available to spend with the Lord, then I urge you to look at how you're living. Something is out of wack!

The rosary was always seen as one of the great vehicles that helped people enter this quiet space with the Master. The beads became for many a way of turning from distractions to His Presence and being absorbed in quiet attention to Him. You could ask someone, "How many decades did you say?" They probably would look surprised and then have to look at where they were on the beads before they could respond. Those who used the Rosary, not as a mechanical thing to get through but rather to put themselves in His Presence, began to find themselves caught up and drawn into that quietness and, when they were distracted, they merely moved on to the next bead. Alas, the rosary became considered as passé— something that old women prayed, but outdated, and in came the Eastern worry beads to replace it. It is indeed incredible, but sad to say, true!

One day I was walking to the Library at the University of Notre Dame, where the Center's offices were located at the time, and was stopped by a student who had been waiting for me. I saw that he had a pair of beads in his hand, and asked him if he had been saying the rosary. He said, "Oh no, Vince, these are Eastern beads, and they help you to quiet yourself. They are great!" When he told me that he had bought them at a steal for two dollars, I informed him that he could have picked up a rosary for much less. We went on to discuss the rosary and discovered that he thought that the rosary meant that you had to say all those Hail Mary's. I told him that was the way it was said, however. People devoted to the rosary would find that it would bring them into this quiet Presence of the Lord, and when absorbed in His presence, the beads then became a tool to stay there. I myself find it impossible to say the rosary, but it is always with me in my pocket. I find myself so often just holding it, moving from one bead to another, bringing me back to His presence!

Since prayer is rooted in life itself and takes its forms and expression from life, it is necessary to always be willing to let go of particular ways of praying. The Holy Spirit will guide each of us and open to us ways of praying that respond to where we are on the journey. They will reflect life itself! As I pointed out earlier, you must never become wedded to one way of praying, because as you grow in the relationship of friendship with the Lord, He will open you to many ways and His Spirit will lead you. When you close down the options, which are so varied and beautiful, and insist on your way, then you run a dangerous course, a course that surely will bring you to the point when you'll find yourself saying, "I don't get anything out of it. What's the use?" You probably will then quit! I can't overstress the importance of not quitting, and the need to be faithful to some time each day spent with the Lord. That fidelity makes all things possible, and in and through that you'll inevitably experience His presence within you and in your daily life. "Wasting time with the Lord" is one thing that you must make a priority, if you want to grow and find inner meaning on your journey. Without it, you'll drift, seek compensations, and that deep inner hunger for meaning will go dissatisfied. Daily prayer is essential, and some time must be spent in it, rather than none at all!

Prayer is also found in the community worship, especially in the sacramental life of the Christian. Father Edward Schillebeeckx, in his book *Christ the Sacrament of the Encounter with God*, says that "the sacraments bring about the encounter with Christ in exactly those seven instances in which, on account of the demands of special situation of Christian life, a man experiences a special and urgent need of communion with Him." He goes on to add that these special situations are "the divine act of redemption itself, manifest in the sacred environment of the living Church, making a concrete appeal to man and taking hold of him in a living way . . . we can readily see that the sacraments are seen in the context of encounter, of interpersonal relationship."[4]

In the past, sacramental theology occupied itself with the individual signs, with the nature of their causality, with their *ex opere operato* efficacy, with the minister, subjects, and effects. Today theology has shifted, and this has put the sacraments into a new perspective. This shift is expressed in the following way:

> Christianity is not a doctrine, it is a person; it is not a theology, it is a history. "I preach Christ," says St. Paul, "and Christ crucified." (I Cor. 1:23). It centers on a unique act of divine self revelation; the Incarnation, life, death and resurrection of the second person of the Trinity. Man, strive as he might, could never attain the grace of union with the Godhead, so God in an act of supreme generosity willed to bring man to himself. This he could have done directly and immediately but he chose a way more consonant with the nature of his creature, the way of visible intervention, the way of

sacrament. The sacrament provides personal encounter with God. In the sacraments God offers to men the
invitation and means of coming to him, and man goes
to God in a welcoming response. The sacrament is the
very condition of the dialogue between the God of
heaven and the man of earth.[5]

The importance of the sacraments in the Christian life
cannot be overemphasized. They are special moments
and are prepared for, depend upon, and can be intensified
by growing maturity of each of us in the everyday acts of
life, just as they may be weakened by everyday acts in
which all fervor is lacking. Thus, the sacrament cannot be
isolated from the everyday ups and downs of the Christian
life.

Since the sacraments offer the Christian the unique
encounter with Christ, they are basic to life. However, in
the day-to-day living, the individual must determine his/
her response to this unique invitation, freely, in order that
it be a real encounter. With certain sacraments this response will vary in frequency with each individual. One
can only point out their importance and encourage others
through a living witness of the Christian life.

Another essential aspect of prayer, which could be lik-
ened to the other side of the coin, is Discipline! Fidelity to
a life of prayer without discipline is impossible. The life of
discipline can be intense, and it must flow from interior-
ity, aimed at freeing us so that we may be open to the
fullness of relationships—with one another, and with God.
In opting for the Christian life, we enter a state and process that is ongoing; we undertake a lifelong commitment
to discipline.

Like other key areas of the spiritual life that we have
been considering, your viewpoint concerning the life of

THE LIFE OF PRAYER AND DISCIPLINE   165

discipline is very important. In the past many of us looked upon discipline, fasting, mortification, and self-denial as quite negative. During Advent and Lent there was a special emphasis on giving up certain things that we enjoyed: candy, smoking, alcohol, and other such things. This practice had as its goal the internalization of the need for self-denial. There were, in fact, laws and rules governing these areas of our life. Paul VI, believing that it was safe to assume that all of us had indeed internalized the principle of discipline, which is so necessary in the Christian life, removed many of the laws and rules. History shows that once the laws and rules were replaced with "guidelines," out went fasting, mortification, and self-denial. It was like taking a negative weight off our shoulders.

For the mystics, discipline (asceticism) was not negative, but a way to open us to freedom: free to be, free to love and be loved. The various expressions of the principle of discipline were merely tools, in order to ensure that we were, in fact, free! If I say to you that I'm just a social drinker and can stop anytime I want, but never indeed stop drinking, then I might well be kidding myself. I might be hooked! The same could be said of smoking or, for that matter, any other thing that we use or experience on the journey. Thus, for the mystics, discipline was that positive action taken to insure that we were *free!*

Earlier I referred to the Human Potential Movement and pointed out that their research showed that one of the reasons that many of us fail to use more than 8–16 percent of our potential was due to poor physical fitness. Christ tells us that each one of us one day will have to render an account for our gifts. If you believe that we will have to render an account, then perhaps you'll be challenged by what they're saying in regards to the nonuse of our potential, our gifts.

If we were to find three persons, all living in more or less the same environment, doing the same type of work, and in different physical condition, you'd see the contrast in a dramatic way. Let's take a first person who happens to be overweight, pays no attention to a balanced nutrition, nor to physical exercise. A second person is one of those kinds of people who never gains any weight, but nevertheless pays little, if any, attention to nutrition or physical exercise. A third person maintains proper weight, follows a balanced nutritional diet, and exercises—the person is in good physical condition! Research shows that the first two use 80 percent of their energy to get through the day, while the third person uses only 20 percent of his/her energy. A 60 percent differential! Can the Christian afford to dissipate 60 percent of his/her energy each day, energy that is essential in living a life of love, a life of friendship?

Yes, we did away with the negative terms "fasting," "mortification," and "self-denial"! Now we have the "in" words: proper weight, proper nutrition, and proper physical fitness! St. Paul describes the journey in terms of running a race. We all know what kind of shape you have to be in to run a race. If God were to come down and line us up for the start of the race, with the finish line bringing us eternal life, I'm not sure how many of us would make it to the finish line—even if it were a short race! Call it by any name you feel comfortable with, the fact that this area of discipline requires constant effort is indisputable. When you lack energy that flows from good physical fitness, when you go home, all you can do is make it to your comfortable chair, pour yourself a drink, and turn on the television. Even then, the television must have one of those remote controls so that you don't have to get up and change the channels—it would take too much energy!

When we come in contact with the God of Revelation

and respond to His invitation to relationship, we enter into a dynamic relationship with responsibilities. Our yes to God's invitation puts each of us into a process of being "clothed in Christ" (Ga 3:27). This process involves us in a life of asceticism, which today we refer to as discipline.

There are many types of discipline, and I won't attempt to give a history of them or their development, but I will confine myself to the task of establishing what Christian discipline is today. Karl Rahner states that "Christian asceticism must spring from the exclusively Christian interpretation of human life in its totality. Man must frankly and existentially accept that phenomenon which casts doubt on the self-contained intelligibility of human life as a whole within this world, namely, death."[6] Our Lord says: "If anyone wants to be a follower of mine, let him renounce himself and take up his cross and follow me. Anyone who wants to save his life will lose it; but anyone who loses his life for my sake, and for the sake of the gospel, will save it" (Mk 8:34–35). It is texts like this that cause Rahner to believe that the Christian practices asceticism, discipline, when he freely confronts this reality, and accepts it by anticipating this death as one goes through life. "It is Christian asceticism when a man verifies that his preparedness for death is existentially serious and inwardly genuine by freely laying hold upon something of the passion of death above and beyond that which destiny itself imposes on him."[7] Elsewhere Rahner says: "Christian asceticism, understood as an existential yes to the God of supernatural life, is therefore a yes to Jesus Christ in particular, of course, a yes to that mode of appearance of grace in the world which unveiled itself directly for the first time in the fate of Jesus, leading him to the Cross and death."[8]

The fact that we have a deeper understanding of our-

selves than in the past means that we have, through the
work of the Holy Spirit, been given new insights into our
relationship with God, with one another, and with our
environment. Discipline, then, may be looked upon in the
light of this relational dimension in terms of promoting
and fostering an environment that will foster growth and
deepen our relationships. It may be said that "a healthy
asceticism does not proceed out of mistrust or contempt
for the body, on the one hand, or for feeling and emotion,
on the other. It is not a process to facilitate repression by
serving as a defense against unacceptable feelings. It is
not a training procedure or therapy. The motives from
which it proceeds should be healthy. It is the mature act of
an adult who, for religious motives, renounces his personal impulses and desires; this renunciation he has accepted and healthily integrated into his life."[9]

From this you can see that discipline is a means, a tool,
to live out your commitment to follow Christ. For the
Christian, discipline enables you to fulfill the commandment of love and to die to all that is or becomes an obstacle to this—it is the work of a lifetime! Without a definite
commitment to discipline, there can be no true living for
others, let alone for God.

The person who opts, who chooses to follow Christ in
the dialogical life, has also chosen a life of discipline. One
need only look at some of the aspects of what is required
in dialogical living to realize that without discipline it
cannot become a reality. Dialogue is an orientation, a
radical disposition which attempts to meet each moment
in openness and love. It is both the relationship between
persons and the very principle that determines the nature
of their exchange. The dialogical person is in communication with the persons and things around himself/herself,
and open to receiving their communication. The follow-

ing characteristics are presented clearly by Ruel Howe in his book *The Miracle of Dialogue*, and he indicates the discipline that is demanded of the person who has chosen to live a life of dialogue.

1. The dialogical person is a total, authentic person. One who responds to another with one's whole being—totally present to the other—one wears no "masks."
2. The dialogical person is an open person. One is free or willing to reveal oneself to another—able also to receive the revelation of another.
3. The dialogical person is a disciplined person. One employs whatever types of discipline that are necessary in promoting the growth and development of relationships.
4. The dialogical person is a related person. One realizes one's dependence upon others, and as one responds to them one is being a responsible person—this takes tremendous courage.[10]

The characteristics of the dialogical person embraces all that we have ever said concerning the life of virtue. Yet it puts it into a language that conveys meaning to those in the world today. It's also clear that this approach puts the stress on the interior, whereas in the past, for many, the stress seemingly was on externals.

We each experience the "tugs" and "pulls" between what we want to do, having chosen to follow Christ, and the nonloving acts that we often find ourselves involved in. This very struggle calls us forth to embrace discipline. Having chosen to follow Christ and live His commandment of love, we must exercise discipline if we wish to remain faithful to a life of love, rather than give way to selfishness and various forms of manipulation and compensation.

As Karl Rahner points out, there is no "recipe for the Christian life in practice, a single recipe for telling with absolute and eternal validity what must be the special gift of each individual,"[11] and thus the life of discipline will of necessity vary from person to person, and from moment to moment. However, without discipline there will be no true friendship, there will be no authentic encounters with others, let alone with God. Hence, one will drift and one day wake up, having related to no one, finding oneself standing in utter loneliness, and the total loss of meaning.

Our mystical tradition states clearly that in all things, except in love, we must practice moderation—discipline. We will also find an emphasis on a holistic approach which embraces our whole being. I've often felt that the mystics would have been very popular with a number of governments today, since they arrived at insights and understandings about life without any grants to study the problem. For instance, the author of *The Cloud of Unknowing* stresses the necessity of good health. He says, "I'm serious when I say that this work demands a relaxed, healthy, and vigorous disposition of both body and spirit. For the love of God, discipline yourself in body and spirit so that you preserve your health as long as you can." And he goes on to say, "Avoid illness as much as possible so that you are not responsible for unnecessary infirmity."[12] Even in the fourteenth century the Christian was challenged and encouraged to stay in good physical condition so that the energy that flows from good health is available to live a life of love.

There can be no doubt that the care of our physical well-being is an essential element of the life of discipline. In the Center for Human Development's Ministry Programs it has been well established that those in ministry who are in good shape find that it enriches their ministry. It is also true that, with most people, the connection between physical well-being and the spiritual life is rarely made. There are many today who have involved themselves in Weight Watchers, health clubs, running, and many other forms of exercise. In my estimation, many of these people would find it enriching to know how important this is in following Christ, living out His commandment of love. The increased availability of energy, along with that sense of wellness resulting from being in shape, fosters discipline in every aspect of our lives.

Even industry today is very concerned about the good health of its employees. Corporations are investing resources to offer forms of physical fitness programs designed to improve health as well as provide recreation. One reason for this new and still-emerging phenomenon is the research which indicates that hundreds of millions of dollars are lost every year to industry in replacing employees who keel over into hospital coronary wards—or morgues!

And that's not to mention the staggering cost involved in sick leave, which is estimated to be well in excess of $20 billion each year. People who have exercised three times a week showed that 60 percent lost weight, and 89 percent reported improved stamina and that work was not as taxing.

The mystics and saints point to the necessity of discipline in our lives, and even have stressed the need for physical well-being. Thus, we can say that just as a daily commitment to prayer is essential, so too one must be committed to discipline each day. Prayer without a commitment to discipline will inevitably fall by the wayside.

Pope John Paul II, in his recent encyclical dealing with

the Holy Spirit in the life of the Church and the world, unfolds for us a rich understanding of prayer and its power in our lives.

> The Holy Spirit is the gift that comes into man's heart together with prayer. In prayer he manifests himself first of all and above all as the gift that "helps us in our weakness." This is the magnificent thought developed by Saint Paul in the letter to the Romans, when he writes: "For we do not know how to pray as we ought, but the Spirit himself intercedes for us with sights too deep for words." Therefore, the Holy Spirit not only enables us to pray, but guides us "from within" in prayer; he is present in our prayer and gives divine dimension. Thus "he who searches the hearts of men knows what is the mind of the Spirit, because the Spirit intercedes for the saints according to the will of God." Prayer through the power of the Holy Spirit becomes the ever more mature expression of the new man, who by means of this prayer participates in the divine life.[13]

The life of prayer and discipline is indeed challenging, demanding, and yet is there any other way? The journey will have its ups and downs, but as long as you never quit, the Holy Spirit will guide you, heal, support, and comfort you on your pilgrimage. As the author of *The Cloud of Unknowing* says, the only other one He needs is *you!*

"THE WINDS OF GOD'S GRACE ARE ALWAYS BLOWING, BUT WE MUST MAKE AN EFFORT TO RAISE OUR SAILS."

REFLECTIONS

1. Identify the significant people on your journey who taught you about prayer. What impact did they have on you? Have you changed your view on prayer? What is your view now?

2. What have been some of the ways you have prayed in the past? Did any of those ways dry up as a source of inspiration and love for God? What did you do when that happened to you?

3. Reflect on the meaning of discipline in your past and present. In what areas do you see the need for discipline in your life?

4. How have you handled failure in the past? Can you identify any steps you would take in dealing with failure as a result of reflecting on this chapter?

SUGGESTED READINGS

1. André Touf. *Teach Us to Pray.* Darton, Longman & Todd, 1974.

2. Basil Pennington. *Centering Prayer: Renewing an Ancient Christian Tradition of Prayer.* Doubleday, 1980.

3. Karl Rahner. *Encounters with Silence.* Newman Press, 1969.

4. Kiernan Kavanaugh and Otelio Rodriguez. *The Collected Works of St. Teresa of Avila.* ICS Publications, 1976.

5. Thomas H. Green. *Opening to God: A Guide to Prayer.* Ave Maria Press, 1977.

CONCLUSION

Pope John Paul II has announced, in his recent encyclical on the Holy Spirit, that the Church would celebrate a Jubilee in the year 2000 to mark the end of the twentieth century and the beginning of the third millennium since the birth of Christ. He states:

> The great Jubilee to be celebrated at the end of this Millennium and at the beginning of the next ought to constitute a powerful call to all those who "worship God in spirit and truth." It should be for everyone a special occasion for meditating on the mystery of the Triune God, who in himself is wholly transcendent with regard to the world, especially the visible world. For he is absolute Spirit, "God is spirit"; and also, in such a marvelous way, he is not only close to this world but present in it, and in a sense immanent, penetrating it and giving it life from within. This is especially true in relation to man: God is present in the intimacy of man's being, in his mind, conscience and heart: an ontological and psychological reality, in considering which Saint Augustine said of God that he was "closer

than my inmost being." These words help us to understand better the words of Jesus to the Samaritan
woman: "God is spirit." Only the Spirit can be so im-
manent in man and in the world, while remaining
inviolable and immutable in his absolute transcendence.

But in Jesus Christ the divine presence in the world
and in man has been made manifest in a new way and
in visible form. In him "the grace of God has appeared
indeed." The love of God the Father, as a gift, infinite
grace, source of life, has been made visible in Christ,
and in his humanity that love has become "part" of the
universe, the human family and history. This appear-
ing grace in human history, through Jesus Christ, has
accomplished through the poser of the Holy Spirit,
who is the source of all God's salvific activity in the
world: He, the "hidden God", who as love and gift "fills
the universe." The Church's entire life, as will appear
in the great Jubilee, means going to meet the invisible
God, the hidden God: a meeting with the Spirit "who
gives life."[14]

It is my own prayer that the preparation for this Jubilee
will foster a reawakening of our great spiritual heritage.
That it will indeed be a time when great efforts will be
made to make known this heritage, which embraces not
only the Sacred Scriptures, but also the writings of the
Fathers and those great men and women who have
formed and shaped our mystical tradition. The present
hunger today, and surely for the years ahead of us as we
prepare to celebrate the beginning of a new Millennium,
is a hunger to experience God and to be able to live our
Christian commitment in a meaningful way. And we must

not forget that we are indeed wounded pilgrims on a journey to the Father.

When I left on my sabbatical I wanted to find a place to hide, where I could study, reflect, and pray. In addition to that, I was seeking an environment that would foster the writing and completion of this book. I settled finally in Florence, Italy. A priest friend and I rented an apartment, a fourteenth-century tower in the center of the city. There are ninety-one steps to the entrance which provide us each day with aerobic points. The tower was fittingly named, by us, "The Hermitage." It has four levels, and the spiral staircase that leads to the top of The Hermitage is another forty steps. At the top is a room filled with plants and flowers. It provides a panoramic view of the whole city of Florence—it is breathtaking! This is where I would go to reflect and pray.

Often, as I looked out on the city of Florence, I reflected that it was here that *la Rinascita,* later called the Renaissance by the French, produced so many classical works of art. It was a city alive and deeply involved in its Christian heritage. Looking out on the Church of Santa Croce, I would try to envision what it must have been like in those days when the Franciscan Friars would fill the piazza with thousands of Florentines to hear the Good News preached. I also became intrigued as I visited churches, each with its own history and treasures of art, and wondered how all this took place. What was the Church like in those days? The Church was certainly "alive," and people were actively involved in the life of the Church.

One day I was talking to a young Italian, and he described for me the Church as he saw it today: "The Church is old buildings and old priests!" When I left him, I took notice of all the tourists entering and leaving the churches—looking at their art and treasures . . . from the past! If you were to travel in Europe, it would become self-evident that in many countries the Church, for whatever reasons, has lost its relevancy to the young and the old. An Italian priest told me that about 8 percent of those who profess themselves to be Catholic practice their faith.

In one parish I visited, the pastor was faced with an empty church and very few participants when he arrived. The church was built in the fourteenth century, an artistic gem, and yet he decided to move out of that building which represented the past. He built a cinderblock structure a short distance from the beautiful fourteenth-century church, and the only word to describe it was ugly. It was ugly! Yet, on Sundays, it was packed with young and old—it is a thriving, worshipping community, and you got caught up in their lively faith. The priest is, as they say, relevant and is among his people, who have responded. He told me that the beautiful fourteenth-century church was not theirs, it belonged to another era! We need simple buildings for our churches today, he explained, and went on to say it was perhaps time for the Church to give away these "gems" of architecture containing great works of art and other treasures from the past. Give them away and get on with the work at hand . . . building new communities of worshipping people, filled with faith, and not burdening this new generation with places of worship that no longer reflect them or are expressions of their faith.

The Church for centuries has been the custodian of these great works of art, and it perhaps had to be, but now might be the time to recognize that society and its institutions can now preserve these great treasures. The churches have become, in the words of one Roman priest, "museums, with caretakers who happen to be priests and religious." Now might well be the opportune moment in history to let go of these museums and undertake the beginnings of a new Renaissance.

When I would return to the top of The Hermitage, I often found myself dreaming about a new, reborn Church. As in the early centuries, the emphasis would be on community and formation. Once again the Church would become "the School of Love and Friendship," where people would learn the art of love and friendship. The priest would be the one who would call forth the "gifts" of the laity so that they could free him, free him to be the spiritual leader of the community, the one who would foster the growth of the individual members and the community as a whole in the life of love, friendship, prayer, dialogue, and discipline, and, above all, open up to his people the wonders of God's love and mercy. In my dreaming I saw an emphasis on people rather than on buildings and structures; an emphasis on love and friendship rather than on doctrine or laws.

However, dreams are far from reality, but wherever I went I found a Church that seemed to be determined to close its ears to the hearts of the people in the streets. Surely they must be trying to tell us something about our ministry? Why is it that the Good News that has been given to us to preach and proclaim to the world, in every ear, is irrelevant today? Is the Good News irrelevant, or are we the ones who have become irrelevant and no longer make sense to people on their journeys? My greatest shock came in Ireland, the land of my roots. Here too, one can't escape the fact that young people are not finding the Church to be at the very center and heart of their lives. While I was there, I was talking to one young man who said that the Church made sense only when the priest was "real" and preached in a way that helped him to live life and follow Christ. He said that whenever he found such a priest, he would go to Mass not only on Sundays, but often during the week. When the priest didn't make sense, he rarely went to church. A mother told me that she could no longer fight with her older children about going to Mass on Sunday. She said that she had tried her best to raise them in the Catholic faith, and now all she could do was to pray for them. She went on to share with me that, for her generation, it was "faith" that mattered, but for the younger generation the Church had to become more relevant and meaningful to them in their daily lives. The same could be said of any place in the world today—if the priest is alive and communicates the Good News of Jesus Christ, and is a builder of community, then people respond.

On May 3, 1986, with the publication of *Sects or New Religious Movements: Pastoral Challenge*, I discovered that my dreams in The Hermitage in Florence were not just "crazy, unreal dreams"; that in fact the Church was indeed listening. The Church, in and through this document, has spoken to the modern world in a powerful and challenging way. It also speaks to the need of change in the Church.

In outlining the reasons for the spread of these various movements today, which also apply to those nonparticipating, nonactive members of the Church, it identifies the reasons for this present phenomenon. I listed four of them in the Introduction, and to refresh your memory, they, along with the others, are:

1. Quest for Belonging (Sense of Community)
2. Search for Answers
3. Search for Wholeness (Holism)
4. Search for Cultural Identity
5. Need to Be Recognized

6. Search for Transcendence
7. Need of Spiritual Guidance
8. Need of Vision
9. Need of Participation and Involvement

The document goes on to point out that, if the pastoral approaches suggested are acted upon, the challenge of the sects may prove to have been a useful stimulus for the spiritual and ecclesial renewal. The six pastoral approaches recommended are:

1. SENSE OF COMMUNITY

Almost all the responses appeal for a rethinking of the traditional parish-community patterns which will be more fraternal, more "to the measure of man," more adapted to people's life situation; more "basic ecclesial communities": caring communities of lively faith, love (warmth, acceptance, understanding, reconciliation, fellowship) and hope; celebrating communities; praying communities; missionary communities: outgoing and witnessing; communities open to and supporting people who have special problems: the divorced and remarried, the marginalized.

2. FORMATION AND ONGOING FORMATION

The responses put strong emphasis on the need for evangelization, catechesis, education in the faith—biblical, theological, ecumenical—of the faithful at the level of the local communities, and of the clergy and those involved in formation. This ongoing process should be both informative, with information about our own Catholic tradition (beliefs, practices, spirituality, meditation, contemplation, etc.) about other traditions and about the new religious groups, and formative, with guidance in personal and communal faith, a deeper sense of the transcendent, of the eschatological, of religious commitment, of community spirit, etc. The church should not only be a sign of hope for people, but should also give them reasons for that hope; it should help to ask questions as well as to answer them. In this process there is an overall emphasis on the centrality of Holy Scripture. Greater and better use should be made of the mass media of communication.

3. PERSONAL AND HOLISTIC APPROACH

People must be helped to know themselves as unique, loved by a personal God, and with a personal history from birth through death to resurrection. "Old truth" should continually become for them "new truth" through a genuine sense of renewal, but with criteria and a framework of thinking that will not be shaken by every "newness" that comes their way. Special attention must be given to the healing ministry through prayers, reconciliation, fellowship and care. Our pastoral concern should not be one-dimensional; it should extend not only to the spiritual, but also the physical, psychological, social, cultural, economic and political dimensions.

4. CULTURAL IDENTITY

The question of inculturation is a fundamental one. It is particularly stressed by the responses from Africa, which reveal a feeling of estrangement to Western forms of worship and ministry which are quite irrelevant to people's cultural environment and life situation.

5. PRAYER AND WORSHIP

Some suggest a rethinking of the classic Saturday
evening/Sunday morning liturgical patterns, which
often remain foreign to the daily life situation. The
word of God should be rediscovered as an important
community-building element. "Reception" should receive as much attention as "conservation." There
should be room for joyful creativity, a belief in Christian inspiration and capacity of "invention," and a
greater sense of communal celebration. Here again,
inculturation is a must (with due respect for the nature
of the liturgy and for the demands of universality).

Many respondents insist on the biblical dimension of
preaching; on the need to speak the people's language;
the need for careful preparation of preaching and liturgy (as far as possible done by a team, including lay
participation). Preaching is not mere theorizing, intel-
lectualizing and moralizing, but presupposes the witness of the preacher's life. Preaching, worship, and
community prayer should not necessarily be confined
to traditional places of worship.

6. PARTICIPATION AND LEADERSHIP

Most respondents are aware of the growing shortage
of ordained ministers and of religious men and women.
This calls for stronger promotion of diversified ministry and the ongoing formation of lay leadership. More
attention should perhaps be given to the role that can
be played in an approach to the sects—or, at least, to
those attracted by the sects—by lay people who, within
the church and in collaboration with their pastors, exercise true leadership, both spiritually and pastorally.
Priests should not be identified mainly as administra-
tors, office workers and judges, but rather as brothers,

ⁿguides, consolers, and men of prayer. There is too often
a distance that needs to be bridged between the faithful and the bishop, even between the bishop and his
priests. The ministry of bishop and priest is a ministry
of unity and communion which must become visible to
the faithful.[15]

The document goes on to quote the Extraordinary
Synod of 1985 and says that "the final report of the synod
notes that the world situation is changing and that the
signs of the times must be analyzed continually. The
church is often seen simply as an institution, perhaps because it gives too much importance to structures and not
enough to drawing people to God in Christ." The synod
placed an emphasis and stress on spiritual formation.

As I reflected and prayed on all this, I could not help but
recall the beautiful and powerful words of John Paul II,
announcing once again that the Holy Spirit is indeed alive
in the Church and in the world today. It is indeed power-
fully evident that, through the Pope's encyclical on the
Holy Spirit and the report on *Sects or New Religious
Movements: Pastoral Challenge,* the Holy Spirit has
placed before us the challenge and pointed the way.

From the report that I just quoted, one can deduce that
the necessary preparation for the Jubilee Year 2000 must
be the implementation of these pastoral recommenda-
tions. Hence, my dream has been given "flesh," with hope
that it can become a reality in our own times—an entrance into the new Millennium, and a new Renaissance!
A dynamic new rebirth which will fill people with the
richness, the reality and the consequences of that incredible event, the Incarnation—the Birth of Jesus Christ!

Another aspect of my dream was that this book, in some
way, would be a vehicle to bring forth some of the rich-

ness of our Christian heritage and affirm, challenge, and give hope to people. I pray that it has been just that, for you.

I return to the title of the book, *Lift Your Sails: The Challenge of Being a Christian.* I know full well, from my own sailing experiences, that there are times when you must shorten your sails. One does encounter storms, high gusts of winds, and similar situations. I pray that you will never pull your sails down completely, but that at least you'll hoist your storm jib and let it help you to stay on course. You'll be able to ride out the storms of your life and the Spirit will never fail you—you will reach the harbor, and will rejoice like any good sailor who finds the safety and comfort in having arrived at a mooring or an anchorage that is well protected and safe.

It is indeed an exciting adventure in following the Lord —it is an incredible call to intimacy and friendship. I wish you well on your own journey and pray that one day we'll meet.

God bless you!

"THE WINDS OF GOD'S GRACE ARE ALWAYS BLOWING, BUT WE MUST MAKE AN EFFORT TO RAISE OUR SAILS."

REFERENCES

Introduction

1. Henry Suso, *Little Book of Eternal Wisdom* (London: Washbourne, 1910). p. 14.

2. Karl Rahner, *Theological Investigations,* Vol. 5 (Baltimore: Helicon Press, 1960–66), p. 139.

3. Secretariat for Promoting Christian Unity, *Sects or New Religious Movements: Pastoral Challenge* (United States Catholic Conference, May 3, 1986), pp. 7–10.

Chapter I

1. William Johnston, ed., *The Cloud of Unknowing* (Garden City, N.Y.: Doubleday, 1973), p. 45.

2. J. Loevinger, J. Wessler, and C. Redmore, *Measuring Ego Development* (San Francisco: Jossey-Bass, 1970), p. 89.

3. *The Cloud of Unknowing,* p. 47.

Chapter II

1. William Johnston, ed., *The Cloud of Unknowing,* pp. 29–30.

2. Ibid., pp. 30–31.

3. Ibid., p. 64.

4. Ibid., p. 65.

5. Ibid., p. 65.

6. Ibid., p. 64.

7. Ibid., p. 90.

8. Ibid., p. 66.

9. Karl Rahner, "The Unity of Love of God and Love of Neighbor," *Theology Digest*, Vol. 15, pp. 87–93.

10. *The Cloud of Unknowing*, pp. 66–67.

Chapter III

1. C. S. Lewis, *The Four Loves* (New York: Harcourt, Brace, 1960), p. 167.

2. Karl Rahner, *Theological Investigations*, Vol. 3, pp. 84–85.

3. Lewis, *The Four Loves*, p. 169.

4. Ibid., pp. 111–112.

5. Aelred of Rievaulx, *On Spiritual Friendship*, trans. Mary Eugenia Laker, SSND (Kalamazoo: Cistercian Publications, 1977), p. 66.

6. Ibid., pp. 71–72.

7. Ibid., p. 72.

8. Ibid., p. 73.

9. Ibid., p. 55.

10. Ibid., pp. 55–56.

11. Ibid., p. 131.

12. Ibid., p. 112.

13. Ibid., p. 72.

14. Ibid., p. 111.

Chapter IV

1. Karl Rahner, *Theological Investigations*, Vol. 3, p. 139.

2. Louis Monden, *Sin, Liberty, and Law* (New York: Sheed & Ward, 1965), p. 31.

3. Ibid., p. 31.

4. Pope Paul VI, *Ecclesiam Suam* (Paths of the Church: First Encyclical Letter) (Washington, D.C.: National Catholic Welfare Conference, 1964), p. 29.

5. Ibid., p. 34.

6. Ibid., p. 31.

7. Ibid., p. 31.

8. Ibid., p. 31.

9. Ibid., p. 31.

10. Ibid., pp. 31–33.

11. Ibid., p. 32.

12. Ibid., p. 34.

13. E. R. Baltazar, "Teilhard de Chardin: A Philosophy of Procession," *New Theology 2* (New York: Macmillan, 1965), p. 143.

14. C. H. Patterson, *Counseling and Psychotherapy, Theory and Practice* (New York: Harper & Row, 1959), p. 143.

15. Martin Buber, *Between Man and Man,* introd. Maurice Freidman (New York: Macmillan, 1965), p. xvii.

16. *Ecclesiam Suam* (Paths of the Church), p. 34.

17. Ibid., p. 34.

18. Ibid., p. 34.

19. Ibid., p. 34.

20. Ibid., p. 34.

21. Aelred of Rievaulx, *On Spiritual Friendship,* p. 97.

22. *Ecclesiam Suam* (Paths of the Church), p. 35.

23. Ibid., pp. 35–36.

24. Ibid., p. 47.

25. Ibid., p. 13.

Chapter V

1. Martin Buber, *Between Man and Man,* p. 35.

2. Ibid., pp. 29–30.

3. Paul Tournier, *The Meaning of Persons* (New York: Harper & Row, 1957), pp. 4–6.

4. Buber, *Between Man and Man,* p. 21.

5. William Johnston, ed., *The Cloud of Unknowing,* p. 65.

6. Aelred of Rievaulx, *On Spiritual Friendship,* p. 66.

7. *The Cloud of Unknowing,* p. 90.

Chapter VI

1. Karl Rahner, *On Prayer* (New York: Paulist Press, 1958), p. 34.

2. Martin Buber, *Between Man and Man,* p. 14.

3. Hans Urs von Balthasar, *Prayer* (New York: Paulist Press, 1961), p. 11.

4. Edward Schillebeeckx, *Christ the Sacrament of the Encounter with God* (New York: Sheed and Ward, 1963), p. 199.

5. Denis O'Callaghan, ed., *Christ the Sacrament of God* (New York: Sheed & Ward, 1964), p. 43.

6. "Asceticism," *Theological Dictionary,* ed. Cornelius Ernst, D.P.; trans. Richard Strachan (New York: Herder & Herder, 1965), p. 38.

7. Ibid., p. 38.

8. Karl Rahner, *Theological Investigations,* Vol. 3, pp. 81–82.

9. "Asceticism (Psychology Of)," *New Catholic Encyclopedia* (Washington, D.C.: Catholic University of America, 1967), Vol 1, p. 942.

10. Ruel Howe, *The Miracle of Dialogue* (New York: Seabury Press, 1963), p. 70–83.

11. Rahner, *Theological Investigations,* Vol. 3, pp. 84–85.

12. *The Cloud of Unknowing,* p. 101.

13. Pope John Paul II, *The Lord and Giver of Life*

(United States Catholic Conference, May 30, 1986), pp. 131–32.

Conclusion

1. Pope John Paul II, *The Lord and Giver of Life* (United States Catholic Conference, May 30, 1986), pp. 103–4.

2. Secretariat for Promoting Christian Unity, *Sects or New Religious Movements: Pastoral Challenge* (United States Catholic Conference, May 3, 1986), pp. 13–17.

VINCENT DWYER, O.C.S.O. is a member of the Trappist community at St. Joseph's Abbey in Spencer, Massachusetts. He has a doctorate in Sacred Theology from Catholic University of America. He taught at the University of North Carolina and then at St. Mary's College in Winona, Minnesota, where in 1972 he established the Center for Human Development. The Center was moved to the University of Notre Dame in 1975, where Father Dwyer developed Genesis II, the first multimedia spiritual renewal program designed to serve laity. In 1980 the Center was finally moved to Washington, D.C., from which base Father Dwyer now oversees its development program.